THE TRANSCRIPTS

THE HISTORY OF TEA
BOOK 2

LASZLO MONTGOMERY

The History of Tea Book 2

By Laszlo Montgomery

ISBN-13: 978-988-8843-46-6

© 2024 Laszlo Montgomery

HISTORY / Asia / China

EB203

All rights reserved. No part of this book may be reproduced in material form, by any means, whether graphic, electronic, mechanical or other, including photocopying or information storage, in whole or in part. May not be used to prepare other publications without written permission from the publisher except in the case of brief quotations embodied in critical articles or reviews. For information contact info@earnshawbooks.com

Published in Hong Kong by Earnshaw Books Ltd.

CONTENTS

Introduction   IX

The Tea History Podcast Part 11   1

During the late 16th century, the Jesuit Fathers became the first Europeans to drink tea. Soon afterward the Portuguese and Dutch traders started poking their noses around China and Japan. They too learn of this amazing beverage and see excellent prospects in their home markets. By the early 17th century The Dutch and British East India Companies are engaging in tea commerce. Though the Chinese at first wouldn't be caught dead drinking black tea, this too is discovered by the European traders and the rest is history.

The Tea History Podcast Part 12   17

As tea did everywhere it was drunk, Europeans were no less enthusiastic than anyone else. It started off with the royals and aristocrats. But once prices came down and the haves and have-nots got to enjoy it, the demand will become insatiable. The Russian tea caravans are also explored. Though their tea culture was different from the ways of the Europeans, Russian people loved their tea no less. During the Qing Dynasty tea just kept getting better. We look at the tea-loving Qianlong Emperor and his contributions to tea culture. We close the episode with the story of John Dodd and Li Chunsheng, the fathers of Taiwan's tea industry.

The Tea History Podcast Part 13   31

The tea trade transforms into an entire industry and becomes the most important traded commodity of the British East India Company. Twining's emerges onto the scene along with coffeehouse culture where tea was also to be had. Over in the American colonies, the Yanks embrace tea as much as the Brits. Milk and sugar with tea became all the rage. And when Her Majesty's government starts hitting up the American colonists with the Indemnity Acts of 1767, the Townshend Acts in 1770, and finally, the Tea Act of 1773, it leads to the Boston Tea Party and an eventual "parting of ways" between the colonists and their British masters.

The Tea History Podcast Part 14   47

Midway through the Qing Dynasty trouble is brewing along with the tens of millions of pounds of tea being imported into Britain. The Qianlong Emperor rebuffs Britain's envoy and puts a major damper on the prospects of China trade. Britain finds the perfect commodity to trade for tea: Patna Opium from India. This ultimately leads to conflict culminating in the Opium Wars. Why this war is misnamed is also explained. This was the age of the China Clipper ships and imperialism at its worst. New black teas are also discussed, including Lapsang Souchong and the one black tea that local Chinese didn't turn their nose up to: Keemun.

The Tea History Podcast Part 15   61

The mid 19th Century brought a sea change to the tea industry. Demand continued to grow all over Europe. China's artisanal tea growers and the challenges of the China market due to all the well-known political and social disasters happening there, raise concerns. The idea to make a go at growing tea in India is seriously discussed. We also meet Charles Bruce, the Father of India's Tea Industry. The botanist, horticulturist, and man of adventure Robert Fortune is also discussed. We close the episode with the exploits of Fortune's first China trip and his discovery that green and black teas both come from the exact same species of plant, *Camellia sinensis*. The famous Guangcai porcelain of Guangzhou (Canton) is also briefly introduced.

The Tea History Podcast Part 16   77

The hero who made Robert Fortune's success assured, Dr. Nathanial Bagshaw Ward, is introduced in this episode. Ward's invention of the terrarium was the one thing that ensured Fortune's hard work in China wouldn't be wasted. We see how Fortune went into China, scored plants and tea seeds from Zhejiang, Anhui and Fujian and got everything safely transported to India.

The Tea History Podcast Part 17   97

After enjoying a monopoly that lasted for 45 centuries, China's secrets of how they turned *Camellia sinensis* leaves into tea are shared with the world (but not by the Chinese). This time we see how the tea seeds, plants, tools, and experts are secreted out of China and successfully transported to the Indian highlands. There a British dream team of botanists and horticulturalists take over the job begun by Robert Fortune and launch the tea industry in India. We also look at James Taylor's efforts to plant tea in Ceylon and how his business savvy partner in this venture brought tea to the world. This partner was Thomas J. Lipton, the one who brought us the ubiquitous Lipton Tea. What a character he was!

The Tea History Podcast Part 18 — 113

In this episode, we focus on the category of tea that is most admired by many tea experts the world over. Pu-Erh tea was introduced sometime during the Ming Dynasty and in time, became the oft-called "King of Teas" for its rich and unique flavor, wholly unlike any other tea produced in China.

The Tea History Podcast Part 19 — 129

Today's Tea History Podcast episode will go from province to province and look at a variety of famous teas such as Longjing, Gunpowder, Huangshan Maofeng, Lu'an Guapian, Xinyang Maojian, Taiping Houkui and a few others. All of the teas to be introduced began their brilliant careers as tribute teas sent annually to the emperor. You too can savor these teas fit for an emperor by purchasing them online at any number of online (and offline) tea sellers.

The Tea History Podcast Part 20 — 145

We continue on with a tour of the provinces, looking at some of the more renowned teas each place has to offer. Teas such as Dancong, Tieguanyin, Jinjunmei, and Da Hong Pao are introduced. Various teas from Guangdong, Guangxi, Guizhou, Jiangsu, Jiangxi, Sichuan, Hubei, and Hunan are discussed.

The Tea History Podcast Part 21 — 163

As Porky Pig used to say, "That's all folks". But only for this Chinese tea history series. I hope you enjoyed this telling of the history of tea.

The History of Tea – Complete List of Terms — 173

INTRODUCTION

The China History Podcast was launched in June of 2010. The original intention of the show was to offer American people a basic understanding of Chinese history. Recognizing a widespread lack of even the simplest awareness of Chinese history in the USA, Laszlo Montgomery used the relatively new medium of podcasting to make it convenient and easy for listeners to access the show snd satisfy their curiosity to learn about China.

Now more than fourteen years later, The China History Podcast is listened to in more than a hundred countries with less than half of the listeners residing in the US. There are over two hundred hours of free content that introduces Chinese history from mythical to modern times. Besides popular Chinese imperial history and post Qing Dynasty history, the China History Podcast has presented hours of content focusing on the lives of Overseas Chinese and their rich history.

The show is listened to all over the world by English-speakers hungry for an entertaining and informative explanation of China's history delivered in an enjoyable non-academic style. So many listeners around the world are Chinese, many of them happy for an entertaining way to reconnect with their heritage.

For more than a decade there have been so many calls from listeners to provide the transcripts to the programs. They will do much to help listeners learn more about China. Laszlo is happy to work with

Earnshaw Books to bring you the transcripts from selected shows of The China History Podcast. These will become a unique and enjoyable way to advance English understanding, perhaps re-learn some forgotten history and gain a foreigner's perspective of China's great history presented by someone who has appreciated Chinese culture since he was a small boy growing up in Chicago.

Laszlo Montgomery

The Tea History Podcast
Book 2 Part 11

THE TRANSCRIPTS

SUMMARY

During the late 16th century, the Jesuit Fathers became the first Europeans to drink tea. Soon afterward the Portuguese and Dutch traders started poking their noses around China and Japan. They too learn of this amazing beverage and see excellent prospects in their home markets. By the early 17th century The Dutch and British East India Companies are engaging in tea commerce. Though the Chinese at first wouldn't be caught dead drinking black tea, this too is discovered by the European traders and the rest is history.

TRANSCRIPT

00:00 Hey everyone welcome back to the Tea History Podcast. This is your host and narrator, Laszlo Montgomery, humble as ever, bringing you part 11 in the History of Tea. We're past the point of no return, so if you made it this far you might as well stay till the end.

00:15 Since we started in Part 1, we've looked at the history of tea from the most ancient and legendary times beginning with Shén Nóng, and how tea cultivation began in Yúnnán and in the Bā and Shǔ States in Sichuan. Then it began to spread to other parts of China along the river systems after Qín Shǐhuáng united the country. Even in this earliest time, although tea still had a long way to go

THE TEA HISTORY PODCAST BOOK 2
PART 11

before it became the beverage we all know and love, the evolution was well under way.

00:46 So we've looked at tea history from Shén Nóng in 2737 BCE all the way up through the Ming Dynasty. We closed last episode with the arrival of the Europeans. They began showing up in the late 16th century and of course they too are going to be seduced by the pleasures of tea and will want it no less than the Tibetans, Central Asians, and everyone else who got a taste.

01:12 Europeans started exploring faraway lands in the 15th century and into the 16th. People were traveling all over the place and many with literary pretensions actually wrote quite a few nice travelogues. Giambattista Ramusio wrote a book about his travels. This one, written in Italian in 1559 just after the author's death, is probably the farthest back we can go with regard to when tea was first mentioned in the West. He was Venetian so traveling was no big deal to him. He's remembered for his contribution to geography and for his book "Delle Navigationi et Viaggi". Voyages and Travels.

01:55 Ramusio served in the Council of Ten in Venice, a.k.a. The Ten. So he was somebody and he got to mix with a lot of interesting people who came from great distances. And Venice being Venice, people from all over the known world came there to do business. Ramusio got to meet a Persian gentleman named Chaggi Memet and better known as Hajji Mohammed. His story was so interesting Ramusio gave him a whole chapter in his book. And in this chapter, Ramusio recalls what this Persian, Hajji

THE TEA HISTORY PODCAST BOOK 2
PART 11

Mohammed said to him:

02:30 "He told me that all over Cathay they made use of another plant or rather of its leaves. This is called by those people 'Chai Catai' and grows in the district of Cathay which is called Szechwan. This is commonly used and much esteemed all over those countries. They take of that herb, whether dry or fresh and boil it well in water. One or two cups of this decoction taken on an empty stomach removes fever, headache, stomach ache, pain in the side, or in the joints, and it should be taken as hot as you can bear it. He said, besides, that it was good for no end of other ailments that he could not remember, but gout was one of them. And if it happens that one feels incommoded in the stomach for having eaten too much, one has but to take a little of this decoction, and in a short time all will be digested. And it is so highly valued and esteemed that every one going on a journey takes it with him, and those people would gladly give a sack of rhubarb for one ounce of Chai Catai. And those people of Cathay do say in our parts of the world, in Persia, and the country of the Franks, if people only knew of it, there is no doubt that the merchants would cease altogether to buy rhubarb."

03:46 Because rhubarb is mentioned in the Shénnóng Běncǎo Jing or Shen Nong's Herbal Root Classic, we know it was present in China for a long time and they knew what to do with it. Rhubarb in its day, because of its laxative properties, was quite a sought after as the Ex-Lax of its day. And, going in the other direction, did you know the

THE TEA HISTORY PODCAST BOOK 2
PART 11

"kao" in Kaopectate comes from the word kaolinite, the very same stuff used to make porcelain in Jǐngdézhēn.

04:14 Anyways, after Giambattista Ramusio's mention, the next time tea makes an appearance in European literature was twenty-nine years later in 1588. Again, it was an Italian writing about tea in Japan.

04:27 *"The beverage of the Japanese is a juice extracted from an herb called 'chia', which they boil to drink, and which is extremely wholesome. It protects them from pituitary troubles, heaviness in the head, and ailments of the eyes; it makes them live long years almost without languor.*

04:45 *The Japanese have as yet no use for grapes, but they make a kind of wine from rice. But that which before all they delight to drink is water 'almost' boiling, mingled with the powdered chia. They are particular about having it well made. The most eminent sometimes make it with their own hands, taking the trouble to regulate the portions and to make the mixture for their friends. They even have certain rooms in their homes reserved for that alone. There is always at hand a kind of covered chafing-dish from which they offer their friends a drink on arriving or taking leave."*

05:24 The topic of our CHP episode 98 was the Jesuit Father Matteo Ricci. All of the Jesuits, when they first began to feel around the edges in China, encountered tea. They drank it and wrote about it. They probably were the first European drinkers of tea.

THE TEA HISTORY PODCAST BOOK 2
PART 11

05:43 | The Portuguese were the first European seamen to ply the China coast. I'm not entirely sure what happened at the genesis of the Sino-Portuguese relationship, but the Chinese showed them the door right quick. But they were persistent, the Portuguese were. Their smugglers and pirates made enough of a nuisance of themselves on the east coast of China to influence the Jiājìng emperor to call for the leasing of a spit of land in southern Guangdong. And their main idea was to herd all these Portuguese into this ghetto. And this, in 1557, became Macao. The Jesuits were formed in 1540. They sent Michele Ruggieri to Macao in 1579 and Matteo Ricci arrived in 1582.

06:30 | As soon as they started to make themselves at home in Macao, one of the Jesuit Fathers Gaspar da Cruz wrote of tea, *"whatsoever person or persons come to any man's house of quality, he hath a custom to offer him a kind of drink called cha which is somewhat bitter, red and medicinal, which they are wont to make with a certain concoction of herbs."*

06:55 | You see, this was all down in the south where they pronounced tea cha. If the Portuguese Jesuit Fathers had tried to establish their base in Fujian, they would have been calling it "tay".

07:07 | In 1582 when Matteo Ricci first arrived in China, the Ming was already not looking too good and would be overrun by the Manchus in sixty-two years.

07:17 | It always starts like this. Someone from afar sees or hears something interesting in a new land. And from the

THE TEA HISTORY PODCAST BOOK 2
PART 11

prism of where they came from, they elucidate on this amazing thing for the people back home.

07:32 Ricci said of tea, in 1610 that the Chinese called this shrub Cia and that they

07:39 "…gather the leaves in the shadow, and keep it for daily decoction, using it at meals, and as often as any guest comes to their house; yea twice or thrice if he makes any tarrying. This beverage is always drunk or sipped hot and on account of a particular mild bitterness is not disagreeable to the taste; but on the contrary is positively wholesome for many ailments if used often. And there is not alone a single quality of excellence in the leaf, for one surpasses the other, and thus you will often buy some at one gold escu, or even two or three escus a pound, if it is rated as the best. The most excellent is sold at ten and more, often at twelve gold escus a pound in Japan, where its use is also somewhat different from that of China; for the Japanese mix the leaves reduced to a powder, in a cup of boiling water to the amount of two or three tablespoonful's and swallow this potion mixed in this manner; but the Chinese throw a few leaves in a pot of boiling water, then when it is tinctured with the strength and virtue of the same, they drink it quite hot and leave the leaves."

08:49 Pretty much from the time Vasco da Gama rounded the Cape of Good Hope in 1497, for a century, all the way till 1596, the Portuguese had the whole Orient to themselves. Hey man, the early bird gets the worm. They were the earliest ones to arrive. So they were the

THE TEA HISTORY PODCAST BOOK 2
PART 11

	ones who got to see tea up close first, purchase it, and take it back to the continent.
09:12	There in Lisbon, Dutch traders would buy this novelty, tea, and take it back to where they came from. The Portuguese didn't have any marketing savvy I guess. Although they were the first Europeans to discover tea and bring it back to the continent from China, they didn't do too much to popularize it. We have the Dutch to thank for that.
09:35	In 1595 though, the Dutch and the Portuguese had a trade spat and Lisbon was closed to Dutch shipping. That's why the Dutch decided to do an end run around the Portuguese and sail to the Orient themselves. They arrived in Indonesia in 1596 and set up a trade center in Bantam in the western part of Java, west of Jakarta.
09:58	And whilst in Asia, just like it was with everyone else, the Dutch people took to tea and knew a good thing when they tasted it. And these Nederlanders were the first to show their fellow Europeans the pleasures of this tasty new beverage.
10:14	The Dutch proceeded to build, in 1619, a trade and distribution center in Batavia which is in modern day Jakarta. There, they traded in spices and used that place as a loading point for all goods traded in China, including tea.
10:30	If you thought traveling the Ancient Tea Horse Road from Yǎ'ān in Sichuan to Lhasa in Tibet was long and

THE TEA HISTORY PODCAST BOOK 2
PART 11

	treacherous, well, the voyage from the Spice Islands to Rotterdam was even more so. How to get that tea all the way to northern Europe in large quantities without any of the spoilage and mold problems that faced tea merchants from the earliest days?
10:54	Necessity is always the mother of invention. This is where black tea was finally figured out. And since black tea is fully 100% oxidized, there's no spoilage, no mold, no nothing. Problem solved. More on black tea later.
11:09	So where was the origin for all this earliest tea being shipped from China to Europe? If I told you from in and around the Wǔyí Mountains in Fujian province, would you believe me? From this picturesque region of Northern Fujian, the tea was transported quite a long distance to the port of Canton, 1,845 li in all, or 900 kilometers. Today this is a 10-hour drive. Back then, it took weeks and weeks.
11:40	You can imagine, along the route, all the duties and cumshaw that had to be taken care of from start to finish. Once the cargo arrived in Canton, the Dutch transshipped it to Bantam where it was laden on board a vessel to Holland. And because they did business initially with Fujian traders, they used the Fujian pronunciation of tea rather than the Cantonese word *cha*. As I mentioned, the Dutch and the Portuguese were first to market. They got naming rights. That's why we in the West call it tea instead of cha.

THE TEA HISTORY PODCAST BOOK 2
PART 11

12:14 | The Dutch were having the time of their lives in the South China Sea and the British were finding it difficult to compete with them. So on the last day of the year 1600, the Queen granted a monopoly to a group of guys for all trade east of the Cape of Good Hope, and this of course became the Honorable East India Company. They, too, were determined to get into the tea business in a very big way. And boy, did they ever!

12:39 | Two years later, after the Dutch got wise to this, they set up the Dutch East India Company and established corporate bases in Indonesia. And somehow they talked their way into Japan to trade directly with them. This was always a shaky deal, and before long the Japanese will show them the door. The Dutch had it good in Japan for a while, even helping the Japanese to kick the Portuguese out.

13:04 | The Portuguese had first landed on Japanese soil in 1543 on the island of Tanegashima, just south of Kagoshima in southernmost Kyushu. Francis Xavier and a few of his Jesuit brothers arrived in 1549. They'll enjoy a brief period in Japan until Toyotomi Hideyoshi kicks them and all foreigners out.

13:25 | Both the Portuguese and the Dutch saw the writing on the wall in Japan and knew where they weren't welcome. So they started looking in the direction of China.

13:35 | 1610 was a banner year in the history of tea in the West. That's when the first shipment of Chinese tea arrived at The Hague. It was green tea, not the black tea that would

THE TEA HISTORY PODCAST BOOK 2
PART 11

soon afterwards become the standard. When black tea starts shipping and after Marguerite de la Sablière in France becomes the first person to add milk to tea, this will later be a good thing for the Dutch dairy industry because the Dutch seized on this manner of drinking tea almost at once.

14:05 And for the remainder of the 17th century, one after another the countries of Europe came face to face with *Camellia sinensis*. By 1635 tea, or the "China drink," as it was known in its European infancy, had already established itself in the Dutch royal court. I read that by 1680, already every home in The Netherlands had a room specially reserved for tea and if they couldn't afford that, they at least had a tea service.

14:36 The Dutch initially purchased a green tea called Bái Háo, which in the local Fujian dialect was pronounced Pak-Ho. I mean, I don't actually speak any of the Mǐn dialects, but it's close to that. The Dutch, like most foreigners, couldn't quite get their mouths around any of these Chinese pronunciations so they called it Pekoe. And as a marketing ploy, and as a respectful nod to their ruling house of Orange, they marketed the tea as Orange Pekoe. And all these years the name stuck. Lipton always mentions on their package that their product is Orange Pekoe and Pekoe cut black tea.

15:15 The Dutch didn't go to China to obtain the tea. Initially it was brought to their base in Indonesia, by Chinese traders. Dutch vessels then transported the tea back to Europe from there.

THE TEA HISTORY PODCAST BOOK 2
PART 11

15:28 Tea is going to permeate these European nations in the exact same way it did in China. It started with polite society first, with the royals and aristocrats. They got to enjoy tea first and this court patronage would trickle down to others in Dutch society who lived on the fringes of royalty and aristocracy. And as it made its way down to the masses, Dutch values and culture blended with the pleasures of drinking tea. And what happened in the Netherlands was the same thing that happened everywhere else in the world. A tea culture particular to those people was born. It's still going strong after more than four hundred years.

16:11 Between 1610 to 1640, the earliest decades of tea drinking in the Netherlands, it remained somewhat of a novelty drink, but as the decades of the 17th century passed, it soon became all the rage in Dutch society.

16:27 And where there is a demand, there are always going to be merchants willing to risk life and limb to supply that demand. By 1675, the Dutch market had been supplied sufficiently enough so that anyone in any major city in the Netherlands could walk to their corner grocer and buy a tin of tea.

16:47 Europeans started with China green tea. Black tea, or hong cha as it's called in Chinese, red tea, began its history in the early Ming dynasty in Wǔyí Shān, again, northern Fujian province. When the Hóngwǔ emperor pulled the rug out from under them, demanding tribute teas be packaged in loose leaf form instead of in its compressed form, the producers in Wǔyí Mountain

THE TEA HISTORY PODCAST BOOK 2
PART 11

needed to find something new to replace their top of the line green tea cakes that had been prized and in demand for so long. I mentioned, because of their value, these tea cakes had a secondary use as a unit of currency. Now in one fell swoop, after the Hóngwǔ emperor's edict regarding loose tea, tea cakes were no longer requested nor considered fashionable.

17:38 Because tea in its compressed tea cake form was readily used as a kind of money, it presented complications to the Chinese state as these tea cakes contributed mightily to corruption in the government-managed tea industry.

17:51 So rampant had the corruption become, some say, this was one of the primary reasons why the Zhū Yuánzhāng, the Hóngwǔ Emperor, why he said, "No more cake tea." His anti-corruption measures at the outset of his reign took the word "Draconian" to a new level.

18:08 How they actually chanced upon the way to make black tea is, of course, the stuff of legends. Tea artisans figured out that after withering and rolling the leaves and bruising them to step up the cellular oxidation, working them with your hands or feet, the process forced the juices of the tea leaf to be brought to the fore whereupon the oxygen in the air mixed with these tea juices, crushed out of the cells of the leaf. And it did that thing it does and the leaves started turning black along the edges and then before long, if you did nothing to halt the oxidation process, the whole leaf was turned completely black. Then the leaves would be fired to stop the process and what you had was black tea.

THE TEA HISTORY PODCAST BOOK 2
PART 11

18:54 | When the foreigners began poking their nose around this part of China, they really took to black tea at once. The Chinese are going to be rather astounded at this because in their way of thinking this fully oxidized, black color leaf was something so inferior to the kind of green teas they liked. Using the banana comparison, to the Chinese, they couldn't figure out why these foreigners preferred rotten bananas, all black on the outside to fresh yellow bananas.

19:25 | Nonetheless, it was green tea that was the first tea to be exported out of China to the West. This was probably Sōng Luó tea or as it's known in the history books, Sung Lo tea. This place was located is in Xiūníng County in Anhui, adjacent to Huángshān, and just to the east of Jǐngdézhēn. Sōng Luó tea is going to join Bohea, Congou, Pekoe and Hyson as one of the other great historic teas that the West imported in great quantities.

19:57 | The good people of Sōng Luó Shān will tell you this is where the first pan-fried green tea was produced in China. Remember, to pan fry the leaves was called Chǎoqīng. Green tea had been produced in Sōng Luó Shān since the early Míng and achieved initial fame for its supposed medicinal qualities.

20:17 | This area will be important later on in the series when we introduce Mr. Robert Fortune. He will take a grand tour of Sōng Luó Mountain and learn all about the secrets of green tea production there. We'll get to this in good time. What a story!

THE TEA HISTORY PODCAST BOOK 2
PART 11

20:33 | One of the legends as far as how black tea came to be grown in the Wǔyí Mountain area went like this. The villagers had just picked their crop of tea and were in the beginning stages of processing it. Then word reached them that some army was about to pass through their neck of the woods. That was always a cause for worry because you never knew if the passing army would wreck the town or not. It was always a possibility that a passing army might ransack a village looking for food or supplies. In this case, the soldiers decided to stay for about a week and the *chánóng*, the tea farmers, dared not make any moves while the soldiers were in their village.

21:14 | All the fresh tea they had just picked was hurriedly hidden under covers or tarps of some sort. And the soldiers, they bivouacked in the village, and seeing these soft covered mounds of vegetation figured this would make a perfect place to flop. So all these many covered piles of freshly picked tea leaves ended up being used as beds. After a week from all the heat generated by these soldiers and all their tossing and turning at night had agitated and twisted the leaves sufficient enough to cause quite a bit of oxidation.

21:51 | After about a week the soldiers picked up and vacated the town. The farmers quickly tried to salvage whatever they could, but in the end, looking at all these withered blackened tea leaves, they considered this a lost cause. But some enterprising person there suggested they rush this stuff to market anyway and see if anything at all could be salvaged from this disaster.

22:14 | Then, as the story goes, there were some foreign merchants, I don't where they came from . They saw the black tea, purchased the whole lot and paid the farmer in advance for next year's crop as well and a new tea was born.

22:29 | It was called Bohea. And Bohea tea is going to act as the benchmark for the rest of the tea trade with China. I myself don't speak any of the Mǐnběi dialect, as I said, but Bohea is a foreign bastardization of their way of saying Wǔyí. And so Bohea it became. For a long time this was the only place in China where foreigners could get their hands on black tea.

22:56 | Later on, even though the tea didn't come from the Wǔyí Mountain area, it would still be called Bohea. It sort of became the Kleenex of black tea. This was the kind of tea Thomas Jefferson and many of the American founding fathers drank and was among the varieties of tea dumped into Boston Harbor in 1773.

23:17 | Other black teas will be discovered later on and will also be exported in massive quantities, most notably Keemun tea or Qímén cha which also originated in Anhui province. This will make a big splash when it hits the market in the 1870s. The other one was called Congou. That was considered the premium black tea. Congou was the name in the local dialect for the word gōngfu, as in gōngfu chá, which we discussed in a previous episode. It was called that because more processing stops were required to work the leaf than with Bohea. Also Congou used the larger tea leaves farther down from the bud.

THE TEA HISTORY PODCAST BOOK 2
PART 11

24:03 | Well, If no one has any violent objections, I am going to do a hard stop right here and we'll review what I just mentioned and then continue this discussion with the green tea of the day which the European traders called Hyson. All for next time.

24:17 | So, until that day, this is Laszlo Montgomery signing off from LA. So glad you made it this far. You may as well come back next time for what might very well be another delectable episode of the Tea History Podcast.

The Tea History Podcast
Book 2 Part 12

THE TRANSCRIPTS

SUMMARY

As tea did everywhere it was drunk, Europeans were no less enthusiastic than anyone else. It started off with the royals and aristocrats. But once prices came down and the haves and have-nots got to enjoy it, the demand will become insatiable. The Russian tea caravans are also explored. Though their tea culture was different from the ways of the Europeans, Russian people loved their tea no less. During the Qing Dynasty tea just kept getting better. We look at the tea-loving Qianlong Emperor and his contributions to tea culture. We close the episode with the story of John Dodd and Li Chunsheng, the fathers of Taiwan's tea industry

TRANSCRIPT

00:00 | Greetings everyone, Laszlo Montgomery here, History of Tea Part 12. Thanks to everyone who gave this show a chance and are still suffering through your humble narrator's presentation.

00:10 | Last time I told you one of the stories about how the Chinese tea makers in the Wǔyí Mountains of Fujian turned lemons into lemonade with the invention of a black tea that the Europeans went crazy for. These became the famous black teas of their day: Bohea, Qímén and Congou.

THE TEA HISTORY PODCAST BOOK 2
PART 12

00:32 The green tea of this age was known as Hyson tea. Along with Song Lo, Bohea and Congou, Hyson made up the four big teas of 18th and 19th centuries global export tea trade. All the China tea clipper ships, all the smugglers of tea, overwhelmingly most of the tea leaving China and heading to Europe, was almost always one of these four kinds, or a combination of them. There were also others, but these were the main ones you always read about in the history books and saw their names mentioned in some of the literature from the 18th and 19th century.

01:08 But it's in the 1600s where all the action begins to happen in Europe. 1610, as I said, the first tea reached The Netherlands, showing up in The Hague. It took a while to spread the word far and wide enough. The German people didn't get to sip their first tea till 1650. Eight years later, in 1658 on the streets of London at Garraway's Coffee Shop in Exchange Alley in the heart of The City, tea had its debut. The earliest tea advert also came out in that year in the *Mercurius Politicus* and proclaimed, *"That excellent and by all physicians approved drink called Chinean's cha, by other nations tay, alias tea, is sold at the Sultaness Head, a coffee house in Sweetings Rents by the Royal Exchange London."*

02:01 These English coffeehouses that were popping up everywhere like Starbucks in our day, served all three temperance beverages. Ukers had a nice quote from 1659 that said, *"There was also at this time a Turkish drink to be sold, almost in every street, called Coffee, and another kind of drink called Tea, and also a drink called Chocolate which was a very hearty drink."* Later on in 1675 Charles II is going to close all

THE TEA HISTORY PODCAST BOOK 2
PART 12

these places down as they were highly and often correctly suspected of being places where men congregated to plot sedition and various manners of conspiracies. As a result of this, most of these coffeehouses would start shutting down and that's when these private clubs began popping up that quickly filled the vacuum.

02:52 | 1658, the year Oliver Cromwell died, that's when the stormy romance began that would last a lifetime. 1660 Charles II returned from exile. 1662 he married the Portuguese Catherine of Braganza. And it is she who we must bow in reverence to as Europe's first true great tea patron. When she took up with King Charles II in London, she brought with her the Portuguese custom of taking tea in the afternoon.

03:25 | As was always the case, no matter the Tang Dynasty or the House of Stuart, popular fashions and new things always started at the tip-top and worked their way down through society. So we thank Catherine of Braganza as the one to introduce this new beverage to the upper crust of British Society.

03:45 | The British had to get it from the Dutch at first. It wasn't going to be so easy for the British to just walk into China and take over. They purchased the tea from the Dutch in India. Then the tea was consolidated on board a cargo vessel and headed back to England.

04:00 | People in the Dutch colonies in the New World by 1670 were already sipping tea, supplied by the mother country. By 1674, though, New Amsterdam became a

THE TEA HISTORY PODCAST BOOK 2
PART 12

British colony and it was renamed New York. It was from that place, with all that early Dutch influence, that tea began to spread throughout the colonies. 1682 William Penn brought tea to Philadelphia. The colonists and loyal British subjects became the next market of people to notice tea. And these future Yanks would embrace it with equal enthusiasm as their British colonial masters.

04:39 In 1684, with China's permission of course, the British were able to get around the Dutch and send their first vessels directly to the port of Canton, Guangzhou. Here lie the humble beginnings of a British trading empire that would shake China to its foundations. These trading companies were after the big three commodities, of course. Always these three: tea, silk, porcelain.

05:06 At the genesis of this trade, the amount of tea being imported first measured in the hundreds of pounds or kilos. Once the 18th century kicks into high gear, British vessels will be hauling millions of pounds of this stuff back to Blighty. And it was the Honorable East India Company who held the monopoly for 150 years for all Far East trade with Britain. They managed the tea business.

05:34 As the 18th century dawned, two markets for China's tea stood head and shoulders above the rest. One was Britain and the other was Russia. Yeah, 1638 or maybe it might have been 1636, Tsar Michael I, the founder of the Romanov dynasty, he was given a gift of 150 lbs. of tea from a Mongolian ally. It started that way. A royal gift, some tribute. And this initial supply, somehow I guess

THE TEA HISTORY PODCAST BOOK 2
PART 12

the upper classes took note of it. Because something like forty years later, a treaty was signed that worked out a long-term trade deal between China, still in the Ming dynasty who at this time were on their last legs, and the House of Romanov or whoever their representatives were.

06:21 The way they carried out this tea trade between China and Russia was via camel caravan. No kidding. And just as you had with the Tea Horse Routes, the *Chámǎ Gǔdào*, that went from Yunnan and Sichuan to Tibet and Qinghai, in Russia they had what was known as the Tea Road. Its history began in 1689 as a direct result of the Treaty of Nerchinsk. They called it the Tea Road because a lot of tea made its way to Russia along this caravan route.

06:53 It was also called The Siberian Route and it stretched from Kalgan in northern Hebei. That is today the city of Zhāngjiākǒu. That was the loading and unloading point in the east. And men and their camels trekked along this caravan route all the way to Moscow. It cut straight through Mongolia right into Mother Russia and then it was a long haul west before these traders were having borscht again. It all began around 1735 during the reign of Empress Elizabeth of Russia, daughter of Peter the Great and Catherine I.

07:29 Russia and China traded more than just tea. There were of course the usual suspects, porcelain and silk. In return for all this stuff the Chinese got furs, textiles, hides, hardware and cattle. It was a good honest business.

THE TEA HISTORY PODCAST BOOK 2
PART 12

Because of the logistics and transport costs tea wasn't cheap enough yet for the Russian masses to enjoy. The still had a way to go yet.

07:56 By 1796, when Catherine the Great left this world, over three million pounds of tea was making its way west along the Tea Road to Moscow every year. That added up to over six thousand camel loads. Russian importers brought in loose tea, but mostly the Russian market still called for tea to be made into bricks, or at least up to the 1770's. I think I mentioned in an earlier episode, the Russians didn't give up their tea bricks too easy. An additional advantage of tea bricks was that in Russia, along the route, in a pinch, because of its intrinsic value, it could always be used as a coin of the realm.

08:39 In fact some of these tea bricks would be molded in such a way that you could cleanly break off portions of the brick to pay for something that cost less than a full tea brick. Sort of like a Hershey bar or the *real de a ocho*, the pieces of eight from the Spanish dollar.

08:56 By end of the 18th and into the 19th century, tea quietly permeated every village in Russia. By the late 1770's, the samovar took Russia by storm and that iconic device became the shining sun from which all aspects of Russian tea culture revolved around. In 1861 there was a factory specially built in Hankou that manufactured tea bricks destined for Russia.

09:28 Isn't that funny how wherever tea went, China, even different regions of China and then to Korea, Japan, Tibet,

THE TEA HISTORY PODCAST BOOK 2
PART 12

Central Asia, the Near East, Russia, and now Europe and the Americas. Wherever tea went, it universally took these places by storm.

09:48 You'll see in Russia, as it was everywhere else where tea came a-calling, all the people from around the world would welcome tea into their culture and then put their own cultural nuances into the pleasure of drinking tea. Unique tea cultures exist in almost every country.

10:08 I said at the outset we wouldn't wade too far into tea cultures that were outside of China. So I don't want to get pulled in by the strong gravity of Russia's rich tea culture. If you're new to tea and want to see what it's all about, the internet abounds with videos showing how the Russians do it and, man, they know how to enjoy tea. Many other tea cultures use samovars as well. In Turkey, Iran, in Kashmir and other places in the Middle East and Central Asia.

10:38 In 1880 came the Trans-Siberian Railway, so you can imagine what that did for the camel caravan business. The caravans and that whole world began to fade until it just disappeared altogether.

10:50 They grow tea now in Russia. I did not know that. Right where they had the 2014 Winter Olympics in Sochi. This tea from southernmost Russia is called the northernmost-grown tea in the world. Someone up there, in 1901, developed some cultivar or tea hybrid that could withstand the weather in that balmiest part of Russia. The tea from Sochi mostly supplies the domestic market.

 THE TEA HISTORY PODCAST BOOK 2
PART 12

11:17 | There's also a tea grown in China near Lao Shan in Shandong province. That's gotta be the northernmost place that grows tea. But at 36.1 degrees north to Sochi's 43.6 degrees north..., the Russian tea is still king of the northernmost teas.

11:36 | Tea didn't stop evolving in the Ming Dynasty. The march continued on during the Qing as well. Like the tea-loving Song Huīzōng emperor, both the Kangxi and especially the Qiánlóng emperor were great lovers and patrons of tea culture. Qiánlóng would hold these very elaborate tea parties right in the Forbidden City inside the Chónghuá Palace where he grew up.

12:11 | During the Qing, the number of places in China producing tea continued to grow. By the time of the Qing, all six categories of tea will be in existence: White, green, yellow, red, Oolong and Pu-erh. The number of tea houses, already quite plentiful in China, during the Qing grew even larger. And the local tea house had become a sort of de facto meeting place for friends and business people to meet and talk over tea.

12:35 | During the Qing, tea house entertainment also took off. Plays and Chinese opera became commonplace in these Qing era tea houses. The dynasty also saw the number of new tribute teas increased more than ever before.

12:51 | If you go to Hangzhou and take the drive just outside of town to visit where they grow Lóngjǐng green tea, you'll see there at Húgóng Temple a separate area fenced off where there are eighteen tea trees. According

THE TEA HISTORY PODCAST BOOK 2
PART 12

to the story, the Qiánlóng emperor himself visited this place four times, to Mount Shīfēng. So enamored was Qiánlóng with the Dragon Well tea there, the Lóngjǐng cha, that he gave imperial honors to these eighteen tea trees.

13:24 The tea-loving Qiánlóng emperor once wrote, "*You can taste and feel, but not describe, the exquisite state of repose produced by tea, that precious drink, which drives away the five sorrows.*" Well, that was easy for the Qiánlóng emperor to say. He drank nothing but the best of the best.

13:46 Traditional Chinese teahouses had been around in one form or another for who knows how long, but they really expanded in numbers during the Northern Song thanks to the combination of all this emerging tea culture, Emperor Huīzōng sponsorship, and the general economic prosperity and good times — until the Jürchens came, of course.

14:10 The whole idea of a nice cozy place to go drink tea, hang out, be entertained, was wildly popular and kept growing, evolving and improving, especially during the Southern Song when the capital was moved south of the Yangzi, to Hangzhou. During the Ming, teahouses sprouted up all over as the common folk also wanted to partake in this pastime.

14:34 China's a big country so it took time for the pleasures of teahouse culture to make its way down to all the cities and towns north and south of the Yángzǐ. But in

THE TEA HISTORY PODCAST BOOK 2
PART 12

the Qing dynasty the teahouse industry was bigger than ever before in China's history.

14:50 A lot of the old ways of drinking tea gave way in the Qing to new innovative ways of enjoying tea culture. The first hundred years of the dynasty was a period of great wealth and prosperity and it reflected in the kind of tea ware that was produced. The kilns of Jǐngdézhēn ran hot for the entirety of the dynasty. One work of art coming out of that place was more spectacular than the next as far as those porcelain pieces destined for the Qing palace.

15:22 Blue and white remained the most popular, but in the Qing, porcelain teapots were produced in more colors and in all kinds of cutting-edge shapes. Compared to the subtle elegance of the Song, some of the stuff coming out of Jǐngdézhēn, especially in the late Qing, would have looked right at home in a French rococo painting. Many of these tea sets were never meant to be used and were only for display. So brisk was the business at Jǐngdézhēn during the Qing, the number kilns increased from twenty to fifty-eight.

15:57 The gàiwǎn, or covered tea bowl that I mentioned in a previous episode, became one of the fruits of Qing Dynasty tea culture. Though it was a Ming dynasty innovation, it was during the reign of Kangxi that it became so pervasive and widespread.

16:14 Tea continued to be used for all kinds of court rituals and ceremonies. And all the way up and down the social

THE TEA HISTORY PODCAST BOOK 2
PART 12

ladder teahouses, both shabby and chic, became places to meet, entertain, see friends, hold business meetings, plot revolution or hang out and compose poetry.

16:33 It was during the Qing dynasty that Fujianese tea masters first brought cuttings to Taiwan and attempted to start growing and processing tea there. Today and throughout the 20th century, Oolong tea from Taiwan has been ranked among the finest in the world.

16:50 They have Mr. John Dodd to partially thank for that. The company he established in 1864, Dodd & Co, pioneered the export of Taiwanese tea to world markets. Dodd used to work for Dent & Company until they went bust. He ended up in Taiwan on some job and hooked up with a Fujianese from Xiamen named Lǐ Chūnshēng. Together these two became known as the fathers of Taiwan's Tea Industry.

17:20 Tea grew indigenously on Taiwan but it wasn't anything good. Tea seeds had been brought from Wǔyí shān to Taiwan in 1855 and were planted in Dòngdǐng, in the lush northern mountains of Lùgǔ, Nántóu County. They grew the tea there, but the critical processing and finishing off was still handled across the Strait in Fujian. Jardine Matheson, the Noble House, began their involvement in the Taiwan tea trade in 1858. Before long, many of these Taiwanese growers were able compete head-to-head with their cousins on the other side of the strait.

18:00 By 1869, Dodd & Co was shipping Formosa Oolong tea to the USA, only four years out of our bloody civil war

 THE TEA HISTORY PODCAST BOOK 2
PART 12

or War for Southern Independence as it's also known. It was a big hit in the US and soon Dodd was shipping his Formosa Oolong to Europe as well.

18:19 Well, you know how it is. One guy sees all the profits being made in a certain business and before long everybody and their grandmother wants a piece of it. Seeing all the profits being made, others jumped into the fray. Some failed and some made a success of it. Some went on to build up the entire industry.

18:39 Well, next episode we're going to shift the focus of our history of tea more to England and how, starting in the 1720s, the demand it started to grow. Though still small compared to peak in 1860, English ships were transporting a quarter million pounds of tea a year to English ports.

19:01 Queen Ann, Queen of England and of Scotland 1702-1707 and then after the Acts of Union from 1707 until she died in 1714, she was Queen of Great Britain. She was the niece of Charles II and the sister of Mary II, wife of William III.

19:21 Queen Ann is going to play her part in furthering English tea culture. She was the first in England to use a silver tea service in the royal household. English coffee house culture, during Queen Anne and her cousin George I's time would really take off. These coffee houses were very much a temperance alternative to the local pub. This English coffee house culture would evolve over the entire 18th century.

THE TEA HISTORY PODCAST BOOK 2
PART 12

19:50 | One of my all-time favorites, Dr. Johnson, he was the greatest of the greats who would inhabit these establishments where all manner of good cheer and good conversation took place. Samuel Johnson 1709-1784 was by his own accounts a hardened and shameless tea drinker. Let's close out this episode with some words from the good doctor who gave us so many great aphorisms and worthy quotations.

20:21 | In Johnson's day, tea was still a "modern luxury". Tea was in demand by the lower classes but it was out of their reach price-wise. In addition to being a shameless tea drinker, Johnson claimed that for twenty years he had *"diluted his meals with only the infusion of this fascinating plant; whose kettle has scarcely time to cool; who with tea amuses the evening, with tea solaces the midnight, and, with tea, welcomes the morning."*

20:53 | When tea drinking began to take root in Great Britain, it was green tea that people initially drank. However, by 1760 more than half of all tea imported into Britain was black tea.

21:06 | Dr. Johnson said of the history of tea in Europe:

> *"Tea was first imported, from Holland, by the earls of Arlington and Ossory, in 1666; from their ladies the women of quality learned its use. Its price was then three pounds a pound, and continued the same to 1707. In 1715, we began to use green tea, and the practice of drinking it descended to the lower class of the people. In 1720, the French began to send it hither by a clandestine*

THE TEA HISTORY PODCAST BOOK 2
PART 12

commerce. From 1717 to 1726, we imported, annually seven hundred thousand pounds. From 1732 to 1742, a million and two hundred thousand pounds were every year brought to London; in some years afterwards three millions; and in 1755, near four millions of pounds, or two thousand tons, in which we are not to reckon that which is surreptitiously introduced, which, perhaps, is nearly as much. Such quantities are, indeed, sufficient to alarm us; it is, at least, worth inquiry, to know what are the qualities of such a plant, and what the consequences of such trade.'

22:22   Johnson also famously said, "*tea's proper use is to amuse the idle, and relax the studious, and dilute the full meals of those who cannot use exercise, and will not use abstinence.*"

22:35   The great with a capital G, Dr. Samuel Johnson. And with that, we'll put the old proverbial bookmark in right here. Next episode, we'll pick up in the 18th century and look at what happens after prices and taxes come down in England and your average worker at mill or the shops or in the mines can finally afford tea. If you thought iPhones were hot, you haven't seen anything yet. So that's for next time.

23:04   Until that time, this is your host and humble narrator Laszlo Montgomery once again signing off from beautiful and lovely Southern Cali. Consider coming back next time, won't you, for another zestful episode of the Tea History Podcast.

The Tea History Podcast
Book 2 Part 13

THE TRANSCRIPTS

SUMMARY

The tea trade transforms into an entire industry and becomes the most important traded commodity of the British East India Company. Twining's emerges onto the scene along with coffeehouse culture where tea was also to be had. Over in the American colonies, the Yanks embrace tea as much as the Brits. Milk and sugar with tea became all the rage. And when Her Majesty's government starts hitting up the American colonists with the Indemnity Acts of 1767, the Townshend Acts in 1770, and finally, the Tea Act of 1773, it leads to the Boston Tea Party and an eventual "parting of ways" between the colonists and their British masters.

TRANSCRIPT

00:00	Hi everyone, Laszlo Montgomery again… The Tea History Podcast. Part 13 this time.
00:05	We're going to look at the setup for some of the historical drama in the world of tea during the 18th and 19th centuries. Although tea made its debut in The Hague in 1610, it wasn't until the early part of the 1700s that tea had taken Britain by storm. And by extension, this meant to the American colonies as well. By the time of Queen Anne, 1702-1714, tea had permeated all the rigid strata of British society. And like it was in China, the passion for tea started with the royals and the rich first. Perhaps it began as a pretentious social function, but goodness

THE TEA HISTORY PODCAST BOOK 2
PART 13

overcame pretension and the pleasure of enjoying a cuppa quickly won over the hearts of whoever came into contact with it.

00:55   By the 1720s, the demand began to rise steeply as awareness about tea set in amongst those who were neither rich nor royal. By 1730, two years before George Washington was born, a million pounds of tea a year was being imported into Britain. By 1760 this number had tripled. And by 1770, nine million pounds of tea was shipped. The population of England in 1770 was only about 6.4 million. So you do the math. OK, I'll do it for you. One point four pounds of tea per person per year, including newborn babies so you know it was probably closer to a couple pounds a year. That's a lot of tea.

01:40   To handle all this tea were a network of thousands and thousands of retailers and wholesalers who got into the biz. By the turn of the century, the average annual per capita consumption in Britain for tea was about 2.5 lbs. per person. Tea had far and away become the most profitable business in which the East India Company engaged in.

02:05   During this early period of tea's development, a chap named Richard Twining got into the business. You know their brand, Twining's. I called it "Twinnings" all the way into my thirties before I got wise. Richard Twining was one of the earliest to notice that tea would make a very civilized alternative to England's normal breakfast beverages. This included gin, ales and coffee, all safer and more healthful than London's own water supply

THE TEA HISTORY PODCAST BOOK 2
PART 13

that was, back then, too contaminated to drink. With tea, the water had to be boiled so you knew it was safe.

02:41 It was the well-known brand started by Richard Twining that played a key role in the early development of the tea business in Britain. And it was Richard Twining and all his progeny who, even up to this day with Stephen Twining, played such a key role during this great historic age of tea in Britain.

03:02 The British East India Company, with the Dutch initially halting their efforts to deal in the spice trade, were permitted, in 1690, to set up a trading operation in Calcutta. The Mughal Empire that had been around since 1526 was starting to show a lot of wear and tear as the 1600s came to a close. Revolts to Mughal rule were popping up all over India. The Battle of Plassey in 1757 put the British in the driver's seat as far as control of Bengal in the north went. They were able to start taxing businesses there and commenced turning the Bengal region into the future cash cow it would become for The Company.

03:46 For the rest of the 18th century and then into the 19th, India little by little fell under the control of the East India Company. By 1772, Calcutta would be the capital of British India. If you're not familiar with the geography of India, this northern part of India, Bengal, was where Assam, Darjeeling, and Patna are located. Assam and Darjeeling, as you all know, was and remains famous for their tea. Patna was where the poppy fields were that would produce the opium that would be dumped in China with historic consequences.

THE TEA HISTORY PODCAST BOOK 2
PART 13

04:24 From CHP past episodes, you remember that the tea-loving Qianlong emperor had banned opium in 1729. And ever since then it had been smuggled into China where dealers distributed it to the increasingly addicted populace.

04:38 Over in the American colonies, tea was no less popular than in the home country. Thanks to the Dutch, the colonists had known about tea since the days when Manhattan Island was still called New Amsterdam. Tea with milk and sugar came later to the future American colonies via France. The Dutch drank green tea straight up, occasionally with some additive for flavoring.

05:04 The Quakers called tea, "the cups that cheer but not inebriate." Someone else had once written, "Tea is better than wine for it leadeth not to intoxication, neither does it cause a man to say foolish things and repent thereof in his sober moments. It is better than water for it does not carry disease; neither does it act like poison as water does when it contains foul and rotten matter." Hey baby, I'm sold.

05:33 The American colonists really liked their Hyson and Bohea tea. They were drinking it in Boston as early as 1670. But it wasn't for general sale there until 1690. By the 1750s it was not only the national drink of England but in the colonies as well. This was partly thanks to sugar that was being grown down in the West Indies. Sugar and tea were linked in the overall trading picture.

THE TEA HISTORY PODCAST BOOK 2
PART 13

05:55 | Sugar and tea went hand in hand in England. Sugar and the slave trade were the front end of what sugar was to tea. The Portuguese kicked off the sugar trade and began exporting it from Brazil in the 16th century. In the 17th century, the British began building plantations in Barbados and other islands of the Lesser Antilles. In the 18th century, the Greater Antilles, especially Jamaica and Hispaniola, also started shipping sugar. Hispaniola today is the island comprising Haiti and the Dominican Republic. In the 19th century after slavery had been abolished in Cuba,1886, the plantation owners turned to Chinese immigrants to work the sugar cane fields of Cuba.

06:52 | Anyone familiar with American history studied the Atlantic triangular slave trade of the late 16th to early 19th centuries. The British would trade their wares; copper, textiles, hardware, guns and munitions to Africa. From these West African traders they'd get slaves. The slaves would be packed up like sardines and shipped off to the New World to work the Caribbean sugar plantations in the West Indies or the tobacco plantations in the American colonies. Of the 88% of the slaves who survived the brutal voyage across the Atlantic, they were traded for sugar, molasses, rum and tobacco. These commodities were shipped to Britain, thus completing a kind of trading triangle. Molasses, for those not sure what it is, is what the British call treacle. It's a by-product of sugar refining.

07:51 | Now this wasn't always the case all the time. Plenty of trade went on between the colonies and Britain directly.

THE TEA HISTORY PODCAST BOOK 2
PART 13

And it wasn't always strictly limited to sugar and tea. I don't want to get sidetracked into discussing the slave trade, but I want to point out that once the Western nations got involved, well, the tea trade sort of lost its innocence. Although the tea business got mixed in with the slave trade only in an indirect way, it was still part of the same daisy chain.

08:22 The Honorable East India Company, by the mid-1700s had sort of fallen on hard times. They'd bitten off more than they could chew in India and managing such an operation became quite a drain on the company. Managing India was the EIC's headache, not the British government's. Aside from that, there was a bit of an economic depression going on in Europe and this also affected the EIC's health. The East India Company was way too big to fail. So when they found themselves in desperate straits, there was no one else they could turn to except the British government.

09:00 Since the EIC received their monopoly in the tea trade in 1698, they had used an army of lobbyists in London to make sure they kept Parliament at heel. They didn't want any politicians getting involved and telling them what to do with their business, so they were masterful in using their money and power to influence the laws and regulations.

09:24 But when they hit a rough patch in the mid 18th century, they had to go to Parliament to seek relief and finally the government was able to use this change in the dynamic to get the upper hand in the relationship. From this point

THE TEA HISTORY PODCAST BOOK 2
PART 13

on, British India fell under British political control rather than solely under EIC control.

09:47 Big business and special interest groups today still use the same tactics of the EIC lobbyists to try and push the government around and to influence the laws and regulations, just like the EIC used to do.

10:01 By the time you piled on all the taxes and fees, legal British tea was quite expensive compared to the smuggled product shipped from the Netherlands. It was very illegal for the Dutch to ship tea to Britain or the colonies. But that didn't stop them. They still purchased tea in China for their own market and did a brisk smuggling business in both England and her colonies. No taxes. Naturally the colonists chose to purchase from Dutch smugglers rather than pay the highly taxed but higher quality British EIC tea. This put a huge dent in Britain's tea business. Thanks to the Dutch, in 1769 tea exports to the colonies from England was down by 50%.

10:49 Parliament's first attempt to deal with this situation was the Indemnity Act of 1767. This gave the EIC a nice 25% refund on product re-shipped to the colonies. This lasted till 1772. But the British government, in order to make up for the 25% loss in revenue, passed the Townshend Acts of 1767. Not only would this offset the revenue from the tax breaks given to the EIC, it would also directly tax the colonists on a number of items. And one of these items was tea.

THE TEA HISTORY PODCAST BOOK 2
PART 13

11:26 | The American colonists were damned if they were going to be turned into anyone's cash cow. The prevailing law said British subjects couldn't be taxed without the consent of their elected representatives. It wasn't the small three pence per pound tax that raised the hackles of the colonists. It was simply the whole idea of the tax altogether. The whole principle began to be fiercely argued.

11:52 | The colonists, being in the colonies and all, didn't have elected representatives in Parliament, or anywhere. So this is where the whole idea of taxation without representation came about. The colonists and the British government were already sparring over this issue and both sides were determined not to back down. So when word got round about the Townshend Acts, this just fanned the flames of discontent.

12:17 | Imported British tea became the symbol of this unfair taxation. Political and community leaders in the colonies began passing the word to boycott tea shipped from Britain. Untaxed Dutch tea however was still getting into the market and satisfying the mammoth demand of the American colonists.

12:39 | After sufficient grumbling, Britain repealed the Townshend Acts in 1770 but left the duty of three pence per pound on tea. This was kept in place not only to show the colonists who was still the boss but also to cover the nut of the salaries of British colonial officials there. But taxes remained in place in Britain sufficient enough to cause a hit to the market.

THE TEA HISTORY PODCAST BOOK 2
PART 13

13:05 | Tea once again became a luxury that was a little out of reach of the lower classes. Demand went down and stockpiles went up. The EIC was again in hot water. They looked to the American colonies and their insatiable demand for tea as the answer to all this surplus tea they had on their hands. The key would be to price the tea low enough to undercut the Dutch who had been undercutting Britain all these years.

13:35 | The answer to this dilemma was known as The Tea Act of May 10, 1773. This gave the EIC the right to bypass British middlemen in London and for the first time, ship tea direct to the colonies. But the three pence per pound tax that came from the Townshend Act remained in force. Some in Britain feared this was going to piss off the tea drinkers in the colonies but nobody listened to them.

14:03 | The EIC began shipping tea direct to the colonies. They didn't have to pay the tax. They set prices to undercut Dutch smugglers and many American merchants who played by the rules, paid the tax for ongoing shipments of tea from Britain. It was sort of a shell game to figure out exactly how the taxes ended up getting paid, but the truth remained that American colonial merchants and by that token all imbibers of tea in the colonies still got stuck paying that three pence per pound duty. The whole idea of taxation without representation was still being grumbled about.

14:42 | Toward the fourth quarter of 1773, a showdown was mounting over this tax. Even though the final price

THE TEA HISTORY PODCAST BOOK 2
PART 13

of the tea was actually beneficial to the colonists, the whole idea about being diddled by Parliament over taxes was really causing unrest. You see, all along, when I was saying the Colonists were all teed off about the idea of taxes being levied without having any say in the matter, the loudest voices by far as far as this was concerned were coming from the direction of Boston in the Massachusetts Colony. Their chief spokesman was Sam Adams and the Sons of Liberty.

15:21 The loudest noise may have been coming from the direction of Boston. But in Philly they also weren't keeping their feelings to themselves. This was the time when words like "united we stand, and divided we fall" were being bandied about. A resolution was passed there at the Pennsylvania State House on October 18, 1773, "the tea tax was an unwarrantable duty imposed on the colonists without their consent; that the EIC was attempting to enforce the tax; and that any person who should attempt to unload or vend the tea would be an enemy to the country." Wow, quite strong words.

16:03 Well, in the lead-up to the American Revolution, it was Sam Adams and the group he led in Massachusetts that caused the spark that lit the fuse that would directly lead to the signing of the Declaration of Independence on July 4th, 1776.

16:20 My fellow Amerikanski's who studied Colonial history all know about the Boston Tea Party of December 16, 1773. This was the ultimate response to the Tea Act that had been enacted seven months before in May. The

40

THE TEA HISTORY PODCAST BOOK 2
PART 13

showdown began in September 1773 when the first of seven East India Company ships set sail for the four ports that were designated by the EIC to act as official agents to deal in EIC tea. This was in Boston, New York, Charleston and Philadelphia. These four places supplied the thirteen colonies with legal British tea.

17:05 About 272,000 kilos of tea was laden on board packed in two thousand chests. A standard tea chest was about 40 x 40 x 62 centimeters, sometimes a little bigger. As I mentioned, the EIC warehouses were swollen with tea and they were anxious finally to turn this inventory into cash.

17:29 Besides the whole idea of this tax, another sore spot with the colonial tea merchants was that the EIC had this monopoly on the tea trade going back to 1698. These American colonial tea merchants... man, so many links were in that supply chain, each taking a hefty profit, and all this ended up getting got palmed off on the Yanks. By the time it reached the homes of the people, the tea leaves had passed through almost a dozen hands beginning with the *chanong* in the hills and mountains of Fujian province.

18:04 These merchants knew all you had to do was sail an American vessel from any east coast port and pick the tea up in Canton yourself and bring it back. That's one way to efficiently reduce the links in the supply chain.

THE TEA HISTORY PODCAST BOOK 2
PART 13

18:19 | I discussed in CHP episode 127 about the 1783 sailing of the *Empress of China*. All the way up to the American Revolution if you wanted to drink tea, legally anyway, you had to buy it from the EIC.

18:36 | Today's tea merchants on the web buy their tea directly from the individual growers of small-scale tea gardens out in the middle of the most remote mountains of China and India. That's about as efficient a supply chain as you can get. Only living next door to a tea garden could beat that.

18:56 | There was a lot of talk and commotion in Boston and the other three ports about what to do about this. They all knew the cargo was on its way and due to arrive in late November-early December. A consensus was drawn whereby they decided to refuse the cargo of tea. Those agents who were cooperating with the EIC were all asked in as forceful a way as possible to resign and walk away from this.

19:26 | The EIC would have no alternative than to *tuihuo*, the word every exporter hates to hear. They'd have to take it back, baby. That's what happened in New York, Charleston and Philly. The vessels sailed into port and the future Americans all got to say a collective, "Get outta here". And seeing how foul and ugly the mood was, the ships sailed back to England loaded with Bohea Tea.

19:51 | But the guy in charge down in Boston representing British interests there, wasn't so willing to bend to

THE TEA HISTORY PODCAST BOOK 2
PART 13

the colonists. This led to a showdown. This Governor, Thomas Hutchinson, was not going to back down and was determined to show a little backbone in the face of the challenge to British and Parliamentary authority. As the standoff continued, the first ship, the *Dartmouth*, was joined by two other vessels, the *Eleanor* and the *Beaver*. The word had gone down the line in Boston to resist any attempts to unload the tea from the ships or pay any import duties.

20:31 So on December 16, 1773, that famous night in American revolutionary history went down in Boston Harbor. A bunch of men dressed up as Mohawk Indians, the local tribe in the area, boarded all three vessels and dumped all the tea into Boston Harbor. Any flights flying in or out of Logan that night would have gotten a bird's eye view of the whole thing. 342 chests of Bohea tea all the way from Fujian province. And with that hostile act, the colonists made a rather extreme protest about who should respect who as it related to self-government and the sacred idea of levying taxes on the people without their consent.

21:16 And later on, after this tempest, other similar acts of protest were carried out elsewhere, directed at tea. There was the Greenwich Tea Party of December 22, 1773. The next year there was the Charleston Tea Party of November 3, 1774. The Philadelphia Tea Party of December 1773 ended with the ship's captain taking the tea back to England. In the New York Tea Party, it ended the same as in Philadelphia. And there were others.

 THE TEA HISTORY PODCAST BOOK 2
PART 13

21:48 | Tea had become this symbol of the unpleasant hold that the British had on the colonists. And so, if I may quote the brilliant James Norwood Pratt from his *New Tea Lover's Treasury*, "En route to sign the Declaration of Independence, John Adams wrote his wife Abigail how he asked at a tavern, 'Is it lawful for a weary traveler to refresh himself with a dish of tea, provided it has been honestly smuggled and has paid no duty?' The landlord's daughter answered sternly: 'No Sir! We have renounced tea under this roof. But, if you desire it, I will make you some coffee.'"

22:25 | I know it's not as simple as that, but if Howard Schultz was around back then he definitely could have gotten a nice chunk of the coffee market right quick.

22:34 | From this whole brouhaha over tea in the colonies came a series of events that ultimately led to the shot heard round the world at the North Bridge to open the battles of Lexington and Concord, April 19, 1775.

22:52 | The sacred tea parties practiced by all the grand ladies of the colony were halted in fits of patriotic protest. This was sort of like the whole Freedom Fries thing. Remember that in 2003? Congressman Bob Ney? Damn French didn't line up behind us when we wanted to invade Iraq. We taught them! Not drinking tea anymore was considered a great symbolic patriotic act that told the colonial oppressors to stuff it. Ukers said about the immediate cause of the American Revolution was the British government's "attempts to perpetuate a tea monopoly distasteful alike to British and American

THE TEA HISTORY PODCAST BOOK 2
PART 13

merchants. Thus England lost an empire to oblige the East India Company."

23:40 Okay. Rather than get started with tea in the American colonies and the demise of the East India Company, let's abruptly and without fanfare just end things right here and pick up next time in part 14.

23:52 Until then, this is Laszlo Montgomery signing off from Los Angeles, California imploring you as I'm wont to do from time to time, to consider joining me next time for another tasteful episode of the Tea History Podcast.

The Tea History Podcast
Book 2 Part 14

THE TRANSCRIPTS

SUMMARY

Midway through the Qing Dynasty trouble is brewing along with the tens of millions of pounds of tea being imported into Britain. The Qianlong Emperor rebuffs Britain's envoy and puts a major damper on the prospects of China trade. Britain finds the perfect commodity to trade for tea: Patna Opium from India. This ultimately leads to conflict culminating in the Opium Wars. Why this war is misnamed is also explained. This was the age of the China Clipper ships and imperialism at its worst. New black teas are also discussed, including Lapsang Souchong and the one black tea that local Chinese didn't turn their nose up to: Keemun.

TRANSCRIPT

00:00	Greetings everyone, welcome back to the Tea History Podcast. Laszlo Montgomery here with you once again, this time with episode 14. More zany antics in the American colonies and with the British East India Company.
00:15	Over on the other side of the world when the future Americans and their British masters were slugging it out in the colonies, the Qiánlóng Emperor was in the middle of his long reign. Some might argue, "overly long reign".
00:28	You'll recall from episodes past that the first half of Qiánlóng's reign was good and the second half could

THE TEA HISTORY PODCAST BOOK 2
PART 14

have been better. By the time he died, 1799, same year but different month from George Washington, his 15th son, the now Jiāqìng emperor, he had the losing trifecta of the White Lotus Rebellion, Miáo Rebellion and an empty treasure to deal with.

00:54 In 1793 the famous Macartney Mission is going to come and go without success. And after attempting the soft sell, now Britain was going to have to force this trade on China the hard way. And into the 19th century they will begin to position themselves for the ultimate collision course that would culminate in the Opium War and the subsequent Treaty of Nanjing and everything else that followed that most famous of unequal treaties.

01:22 But the thing about the Opium War is that it's sort of misnamed. The root cause of the Opium War wasn't *Papaver somniferum, or opium*. It was *Camellia sinensis*.... the very subject of this podcast show. I maintain, to be more accurate, this should have been called The Tea War, not the Opium War. Why's that?

01:46 You've perhaps heard it before in high school or college history and in an old CHP episode on the Opium War. Not to mention also in the History of Hong Kong series and that Qing Dynasty overview. The thing that made the whole mechanics of China trade so odious was that the British traders were forced to put up with this hated Canton System. This had been put in place by the Kangxi Emperor back in 1687. The Qiánlóng emperor in 1757 made things even worse by forcing the foreign traders to all deal with the Hoppo and the whole corrupt

THE TEA HISTORY PODCAST BOOK 2
PART 14

CoHong in Canton.

02:26 These were the officials appointed by the emperor to have exclusive rights to fleece the foreign traders and make them pay a little extra to carry out commerce in China.

02:37 You know the boilerplate story. The British didn't have a whole hell of a lot of commodities or luxuries to sell to the Chinese to offset the massive amount of tea purchases required to satisfy the home markets. As the 18th century ended and the 19th century began, the British Isles had become thoroughly and hopelessly addicted to this beverage. And having a grossly unfavorable balance of trade with China, England couldn't offer enough to offset the tea purchases. Therefore they had to pay the shortfall in silver bullion and it was wrecking their economy.

03:16 So in order to reverse this grossly unfavorable trade balance, the East India Company started dumping all this made-in-India opium into the Chinese market. And opium, when used as a narcotic drug, like all narcotics and opioid drugs, not that I've ever tried it or anything, but I hear its very addictive. And that was indeed the case in China and widespread addiction to opium predictably followed into the first half of the 19th century.

03:45 So Indian-grown opium took hold in the China market amongst the richest and poorest citizens. That balanced things out nicely with respect to the tea trade and so

 THE TEA HISTORY PODCAST BOOK 2
PART 14

widespread was the opium use in China, silver bullion reversed course and was now flowing in the opposite direction out of China's economy and into Britain's.

04:08 And now, with the tables turned, the Qing government had to figure out some way to halt this disastrous trade imbalance.

04:17 I don't want to repeat the whole Lín Zéxú story and re-tell the story of the Opium War again here. But suffice to say, when the Dàoguāng Emperor put his foot down and demanded no more opium be imported into China, Britain's response was, well, the Opium War.

04:36 And when that ended and after China had been soundly defeated, what followed was the Treaty of Nanjing, the first of many bùpíngděng tiáoyuē or Unequal Treaties to follow. And believe me, even though this happened eighteen decades ago, in the minds of many people in China, leaders and common people alike, it's like it happened yesterday.

05:01 And with this treaty, the East India Company finally had what it had always wanted, the end of the Canton System and their very own base of operations to carry out trade. And this base was of course, the new British Crown Colony of Hong Kong.

05:19 So although we know this historical incident as the Opium War, it's safe to say that had it not been for the trade imbalance due to the tea addiction of the Europeans, there wouldn't have been such an urgency

THE TEA HISTORY PODCAST BOOK 2
PART 14

to dump all this Patna opium in the Chinese market.

05:37 Well, Opium War, Tea War, the outcome still reverberates into our 21st century times.

05:47 In 1823, something ominous happened when the British had discovered tea growing wild in Assam. It's going to take a long time to figure out how to turn this indigenous Assam leaf into a marketable product, but figure it out they did. And in the next couple episodes we'll see how they accomplished that.

06:09 Prior to the Opium War and subsequent treaty, in 1834, The East India Company had lost its monopoly on tea. And even with the loss of this monopoly, the Company had still resisted trying to take advantage of their favorable situation in India to explore whether tea, their number one business far and away, could be cultivated there.

06:32 But with the market evolving like it was, still going nowhere but up, the British East India Company lit a fire under that notion. And growing tea in India on a mass scale, started to get more serious discussion. By 1844, following the opening of all these treaty ports in China as a result of the Treaty of Nanjing, 53 million lbs. of tea had been shipped to England.

07:00 Before we move on to early efforts to cultivate tea in India, let me quote again from James Norwood Pratt, the "New Tea Lover's Treasury" about the final legacy of the East India Company. This has always been one

THE TEA HISTORY PODCAST BOOK 2
PART 14

of my favorite bits of his tea writing. He said that The Company had come

07:20

"to be hated and loathed by smugglers and consumers alike as a symbol of corrupt, complacent monopoly. But it also founded the cities of Calcutta, Bombay, Singapore and Hong Kong. It hired Captain Kidd to combat piracy and made Elihu Yale a fortune with which to endow a university. Its corporate structure is the model for all joint-stock companies to this day. The Stars and Stripes was inspired by its flag, the 'typical' New England church patterned after its London chapel, and St. Petersburg modeled on its shipyards where Czar Peter the Great had worked incognito. It created British India, caused the Boston Tea Party and kept Napoleon captive on its island possession St. Helena. And this long-standing effort and enterprise was chiefly paid for by tea. The Company's fortunes came to rest on products destined to go down the drain in Europe and up in smoke in Asia."

08:25   James Norwood Pratt, ladies and gentlemen.

08:29   A lot of people had discussed this for years, giving a go at planting and cultivating tea in India. The more the years passed, the more viable the project became. But too little was known about the tricks of the trade. Too many things remained secret that only the Chinese seemed to know. I mentioned already turning *Camellia sinensis* leaves into tea is not an intuitive process at all. We already saw how many centuries it took Chinese tea farmers to figure out the secrets.

THE TEA HISTORY PODCAST BOOK 2
PART 14

09:00 | And even with the opening of the treaty ports and foreigners running around amok in these cities, all the secrets of manufacturing tea, the way they loved it in Europe and elsewhere... those secrets were deep in the mountains and hills, distant from these newly opened cities. We're going to get to this next time.

09:19 | This period in the history of tea, the 1830s to the 185's, this was also the age of the China tea clippers and the fabled annual tea races every April. This was a race between the first clipper ships sailing out of the ports of Fujian to England. Whoever was the first to market in England with this freshest first flush tea of the season, the most prized quality of all, would reap a fortune in prestige and premiums paid for their product. These ships were fast enough to make the voyage non-stop in about eighty-five days.

09:57 | A quick word about the flush. This is the most expensive and sought-after part of the tea plant. A single flush equals the flower bud and the two youngest leaves. The leaves below the flush are still used, but the flush is the most prized and contains the freshest of flavors. On a lot of these online tea sites, you'll see this word a lot.

10:20 | How many of you might remember this period of the China Clippers? And how they were portrayed so memorably in James Clavell's book "Taipan". Not only was this period in history the time of Dirk Struan and the Noble House, it was the peak time of the Yankee Clippers, the China Clippers, Donald McKay, James Baines, the British Tea Clippers, The Thermopylae, the

THE TEA HISTORY PODCAST BOOK 2
PART 14

Cutty Sark and the Great Tea Race of 1866.

10:49 The history of tea during the late Ming and throughout the Qing dynasty was a raucous one. China still held a very strong competitive advantage, having a monopoly and all. To engage in the tea business with them, the China tea merchants dictated very favorable terms for themselves and took very healthy profits along the China-side of the supply chain.

11:13 But as unfavorable as the trade terms may have been for the British, now thanks to the opium trade, once again, tea was an immensely profitable business for the East India Company and by extension the British Exchequer who got a piece of that action for a long while.

11:31 China had enjoyed a nice monopoly on the world tea supply. In the 19th century during the reign of the Dàoguāng Emperor, someone who we'll look at next episode is going to carry out a little industrial espionage financed by The Honorable Company, the good old EIC, to steal not only the hardware for producing tea but the software as well.

11:55 There was a very strict ban in place during the Qing dynasty prohibiting the export of live tea plants. But despite this ban, for the first time since the most ancient times of Shénnóng, 2737 BCE, China's monopoly on tea and more importantly the secret manufacturing process was about be broken.

THE TEA HISTORY PODCAST BOOK 2
PART 14

12:19   Again, all for next episode. Tea by the time of the mid-Qing is totally recognizable to us. Teabags haven't been invented yet. That won't come until the 1920s. But loose leaf teas sold in a surfeit of beautifully designed tins, and porcelain tea pots, and tea cups of Chinese design and chinoiserie, were as common as sugar and milk in most parts of Europe and certainly in the UK and her colonies. And the kilns of Jǐngdézhēn down in Northern Jiāngxī province were going full-boat throughout the 19th century supplying the worldwide demand for their wares.

13:01   You know in our 21st century world we can choose from hundreds of the perhaps thousands of different kinds of teas made around the world. Choices abound. But in the days when Westerners were all clamoring for tea in China, the 1600s clear through till the end of the 1800s, they didn't have as many choices. I mentioned Bohea tea as the standard benchmark black tea of its day. There was also Congou which was considered a step-up in quality. I think I mentioned Congou tea was what many of us know as the dark gongfu tea.

13:35   Let me mention one more prized tea from back in the day. And if you've never tried it yourself perhaps your grandmother or great-grandmother, if she wasn't a member of the LDS Church that is, might have had this in her pantry. It's called Lapsang Souchong tea. In Mandarin this would be pronounced Lìshān Xiǎozhǒng. It's known today as Zhèngshān Xiǎozhǒng. It's a kind of tea from the Wǔyí Mountain region where Bohea comes from.

 THE TEA HISTORY PODCAST BOOK 2
PART 14

14:03 | If you remember from Part 11, the story of how black tea came about, well, another version of that story is directly related to this discovery of Lapsang Souchong tea. This was during the Ming Dynasty. Same story. Soldiers invaded a village where they were producing tea and thanks to stopping production and burying all the leaves under tarps. By the time the soldiers came and went, the green tea leaves buried underneath all these covers or tarps, had all turned black.

14:34 | The Lapsang Souchong version of the story says that prior to the farmers hiding the leaves underneath the covers, they quickly dried them first and they did this by exposing the tea leaves to hot smoke.

14:46 | And that's the distinguishing characteristic about Lapsang souchong tea. It's all in the processing. The drying is carried out by burning the pinewood logs that were local to the area. The smoke from this pinewood is absorbed into the leaves and what you have is a black tea with a unique smoky flavor. So this tea also was another standard in the repertoire of teas that China shipped to the West. Today, everybody makes it. Twinings, Harney & Sons, Taylors, Fortnum & Mason and dozens of other lesser known but no doubt distinguished brands.

15:24 | This is one of those teas that's sort of an acquired taste. These smokey teas are called Xūnchá. To Xūn something is to smoke it. I wasn't a big fan at first, but I started liking Keemun Tea. Remember way back in those days, Chinese sort of looked down on black teas as purely a foreigner thing. And, no pun intended, it wasn't their cup of tea.

15:50 I just mentioned Keemun Tea. Once Keemun tea was introduced to the market, growers in China began to make black tea respectable and palatable enough to be accepted in the China domestic market. Keemun, Kay-moon, was Cantonese for Qímén, a city in Anhui Province near the gorgeous granite peaks of Yellow Mountain, Huáng shān. The tea masters from in and around Keemun or Qímén put out several teas that all carried the Keemun name. It made its debut in the first year of the Guāngxù Emperor's reign in 1875.

16:29 Keemun is a black tea. Some call it the "Queen of Black Teas" and the "Bordeaux of Teas". The person in Anhui who developed this tea first learned how to make Congou down in Fujian. He just brought the know-how back to his home in Qímén, Anhui province.

16:49 This tea goes by many names and there were many varieties that came out of the four main growing areas around Qímén. Keemun Háo Yá, Keemun Máoféng, Keemun Congou and others. This is the only black tea in China that rose to the level of Tribute Tea status. You can bet the Guāngxù emperor sipped this tea as he stressed out over the state of the Qing Dynasty during his watch.

17:20 But it sure was popular in England. Keemun tea leaves ended up as one of the base teas in your typical English Breakfast teas. You brew it at 90 degrees Celsius, 194 F for two to five minutes depending. The color of the tea, the liquor as the industry insiders say, will have a reddish color. Depending on the terroir of that particular Keemun tea, it'll give off either a floral, fruity or a smoky

THE TEA HISTORY PODCAST BOOK 2
PART 14

scent. This is a very delicate tea even though it's a black tea. Keemun black tea uses only the whole bud set just like many high-end green teas. That's why it doesn't look as course as other whole leaf black teas.

18:05 Next episode we'll look at how the British were able to figure out the whole tea processing thing and as a result of this, they were able to launch the Indian and Sri Lankan tea industry. That's quite a story and rather than get started in this episode, we're going to save that until next time.

18:22 Quite a history tea has. Would you agree? From a bitter tasting brew sharing a Chinese character tú with *kǔcài*, a bitter vegetable. From those Bronze Age times to the Han, the Sui, the Tang, Song, Ming, tea just kept getting better and better.

18:43 Because of the way geography and exploration was, at first it was all those peoples adjacent to China where the Silk Roads passed through who learned about tea first. When boats started sailing on the seven seas in the 15th and 16th centuries, Westerners too got to see and taste for the first time this beverage called *tay* on the east coast of China and *chá* in the south.

19:10 This was quite a dynamic and explosive age when Great Britain and the colonies so quickly fell in love with tea. Who was to know what all the future blowback would be from the Seven Years War, the finances of the East India Company at the time, the matter of taxes derived from the tea trade, China's continued monopoly on tea know-

THE TEA HISTORY PODCAST BOOK 2
PART 14

how and technology. It's funny to see how everything was related to everything and tea was caught in the middle of it all.

19:40 As for the tea dictionaries, encyclopedias, guidebooks that give you the skinny on each and every tea readily available in the market, resources abound. There are books galore that go tea by tea and explain about where it comes from, how to brew it, what water temperature to use, the whole works. There are books. There are tea web sites. YouTube Channels. I had no idea. And if this isn't enough to satisfy your soul, on top of all these resources there are experts in the tea blogosphere who can teach you even more.

20:17 OK, class dismissed a little earlier than usual.

20:20 This is Laszlo Montgomery signing off from Los Angeles, California. Please continue to stick with the program and consider joining me next time perhaps for another piquant episode of the Tea History Podcast.

The Tea History Podcast
Book 2 Part 15

THE TRANSCRIPTS

SUMMARY

The mid 19th Century brought a sea change to the tea industry. Demand continued to grow all over Europe. China's artisanal tea growers and the challenges of the China market due to all the well-known political and social disasters happening there, raise concerns. The idea to make a go at growing tea in India is seriously discussed. We also meet Charles Bruce, the Father of India's Tea Industry. The botanist, horticulturist, and man of adventure Robert Fortune is also discussed. We close the episode with the exploits of Fortune's first China trip and his discovery that green and black teas both come from the exact same species of plant, *Camellia sinensis*. The famous Guangcai porcelain of Guangzhou (Canton) is also briefly introduced.

TRANSCRIPT

00:00 | Hey everyone Laszlo Montgomery again. Part 15 today of our Tea History Podcast. Thanks again to everyone who has made it this far.

00:11 | At the very outset of this series, all those episodes ago, we looked at the second of the mythical Three Sovereigns of the most ancient times. I won't say his name. You all know who Shén Nóng is by now. Starting from around his time in pre-Bronze Age China all the way into the mid 19th century, the Middle Kingdom had enjoyed a most profitable worldwide monopoly on the growing,

THE TEA HISTORY PODCAST BOOK 2
PART 15

processing and export of tea.

00:39 Thanks in part to their long and continuous civilization, the Chinese, over more than forty centuries, from 2737 BCE all the way up to and during the Qing dynasty, 1644-1911, had gradually figured out almost every conceivable way to eke out as much goodness and pleasure as could be had from this *Camellia sinensis* plant. China acted as the fountainhead or yuántóu in both the growing of tea and in the development and refinement of tea culture.

01:15 Over the millennia, countless new cultivars had been developed in all the tea growing regions of China that used selective breeding or hybridization. When you read today that there exist thousands of different kinds of teas in the market, it's from this method that so many varieties were created.

01:35 You see, that was the thing about tea, or any plant for that matter. As long as the growing conditions were suitable, you could grow tea. As long as you had the smarts and technology to process the tea leaves, the only other thing you needed were the right growing conditions. Today, tea is now grown in more than fifty countries and because of all the advances in horticulture and plant genetics, tea plants thrive in places where it was once unthinkable to grow. Tea's even grown on the Island of Jersey in the English Channel. Even in Scotland in Perthshire, Fife and Angus they're growing tea.

02:15 But back in the 19th century, they lacked the technologies and wherewithal to stray too far from the natural tea

THE TEA HISTORY PODCAST BOOK 2
PART 15

gardens that ran from the Brahmaputra Valley to Eastern China.

02:27 As early as 1788 Sir Joseph Banks, an English naturalist, had been the first to suggest the notion of growing tea in India. That's what today's episode is all about. Taking a plant from China and transporting it to India where the growing conditions were also equally ideal.

02:48 But it wasn't enough just to plant the seeds and start growing tea. After fifteen episodes we've learned, It was slightly more complicated than that. During the Macartney Mission to China, British had been able to secure some seeds and brought them back to Calcutta, but nothing came of that.

03:08 Planting and harvesting the tea leaves was one thing. That was only the front end of the whole process. So many steps followed this part. And what those steps were, even in the 19th century, remained a mystery to the British eager to get into the tea cultivation business themselves.

03:27 When the East India Company bosses and other trading companies first had the idea to create an Indian tea industry. They knew the final product that they sold would have to taste just as good as the China stuff. That was the fundamental problem. As I said at the outset of this series, turning raw tea leaves into a fine tasting beverage wasn't an intuitive process at all. It had taken the Chinese thousands of years of trial and error and ingenuity to get it right.

THE TEA HISTORY PODCAST BOOK 2
PART 15

03:59 | Early on, British tea traders familiar with Bengal in northeast India wondered if this could be done. Their first big break came in 1823.

04:11 | Soldier and adventurer Robert Bruce, a Scotsman, provided the breakthrough that started everything. This was not Robert the Bruce, King of Scots from 1306-1329. He was one of those many Brits who came to India in colonial days to make something of his life. Whilst up in northern Assam he came into contact with a nobleman of those parts named Maniram Dewan who in turn introduced him to the Singhpho tribal headman up there named Bessa Gam. That's how it all began.

04:47 | Robert Bruce, trained in botany, observed the local people consuming the leaves that he was pretty sure were *Camellia sinensis*. This was the great moment. This was where Robert Bruce had the idea that if what he was seeing was in fact true, there was a pretty good chance the British could grow tea in this land.

05:09 | The Singhpho tribal leader Bessa Gam assured Robert Bruce that next time he returned he would be happy to offer him both seeds and tea plants for his study.

05:20 | What Robert Bruce chanced up was the Assam leaf varietal of the *Camellia sinensis* plant. It was he who discovered what the local Indians probably had known about since time immemorial.

05:34 | Robert Bruce died the following year in 1824. Fortunately the secret of the location of these tea gardens and the

THE TEA HISTORY PODCAST BOOK 2
PART 15

indigenous tea plants in Assam didn't die with him. Alas, Robert Bruce's brother Charles was there to pick up the ball and carry it forward.

05:53 Charles Alexander Bruce, not a well-known name perhaps, but he's called the Father of the Indian Tea Industry. After his brother turned him on to these tea plants and the location in Assam where he found them growing indigenously, he went to this location given to him by his brother Robert and met with the same chieftain who, true to his word, provided Charles Bruce with the sample seeds and plants. And that's really all it took. In that moment, the monopoly China enjoyed all those thousands of years was suddenly put in jeopardy.

06:30 He brought these specimens back to where he was living near the source of the Brahmaputra River in northeast India. There he planted the seeds and plants and waited for nature to do its thing.

06:43 And the upshot was the formation of an aptly named Tea Committee in 1834. They were based in Calcutta and tasked with managing this whole enterprise of possibly growing tea in India. Charles Bruce, in a report he sent to this esteemed committee in 1839 stated, "The difficulty of carrying on dealings with China, which seems to be always increasing, has of late years led to an anxious discussion of the possibility of obtaining tea from a different source."

07:18 The British had been trying in vain to steal tea plants and seeds from China since the 1760s. Back then in the pre-

THE TEA HISTORY PODCAST BOOK 2
PART 15

treaty-port days, it was difficult, if not impossible for a Westerner to get around China. Besides that difficulty, there was also the matter of handling the stolen tea plants and transporting them over a great distance. Though this technology will be figured out in time, the whole idea of transplanting the tea plants from Anhui to Assam, as the Macartney Mission learned, the time hadn't come yet. It was like trying to bring moon rocks back to planet earth in the 1950s. The vision was there, but not the means.

08:02 The East India Company had already contracted Charles Bruce in 1835 to lead this effort of jump-starting the planting and growing of tea in Assam. He was made Superintendent of all the Tea Plantations there. By 1836 he was already sending samples to the Tea Committee. It was judged to be not bad. The following year, a much greater quantity was sent and ended up selling at auction in London in 1839.

08:31 So the research began on how to turn this *Camellia sinensis* varietal Assamica into a beverage that the British public would allow into their homes and teapots. With the EIC monopoly on tea now gone, The Company was very hot to get this Indian operation up and running so that they could say goodbye and good riddance to their China suppliers.

08:58 Well, easier said than done. Without the benefits of everything we know today and all the tools at our disposal, it was slow going. But no one had given up hope yet of the holy grail, transplanting Chinese plants

THE TEA HISTORY PODCAST BOOK 2
PART 15

from Anhui, Zhejiang or Fujian and replanting them in their experimental plantations in India.

09:21　And to that end, let's begin looking at the life of Mr. Robert Fortune. He was another Scotsman from Berwickshire, fifty miles east of Edinburgh. He was born in the year 1812, the time of the Jiāqìng emperor in China.

09:37　Fortune's period in China would be spent mostly during the Dàoguāng and Xiánfēng eras. After so many past episodes, we all know whenever we hear the names of those two emperors, it always evokes the baddest of the bad old days of Western imperialism and domination in China. You almost know in advance whatever happens during those two eras, it doesn't end well for China.

10:03　In looking at the history of tea like we've done, all these past episodes, we've seen how China led the world in not only discovering tea but also figuring out all the health benefits and best ways to prepare it. Japan, Korea, Tibet, Southeast Asia, Central Asia and beyond all embraced this drink.

10:24　After Islam had taken hold in Central Asia and of course in the Middle East and North Africa, adherents were no longer permitted to partake in the daily tipple. But tea was there, waiting in the wings to act as a fine replacement to wine and spirits.

10:42　I think I mentioned last episode, by the Qing dynasty all the six main categories of tea had by this time already been discovered. Mechanization had been able to

 THE TEA HISTORY PODCAST BOOK 2
PART 15

replace some of the hand work, but Chinese teas were still mainly a hand-made industry. Tea was by then well on its way to becoming the world's second most consumed substance after water.

11:06 Also around this time in the Qīng, tea ware became more beautiful, more fanciful and at the high-end, more spectacular. I remember on one of my Guangzhou trips I visited the Guǎngdōng Museum and saw a fantastic exhibit on Guāngcǎi porcelain. Guāngcǎi is the abbreviated term for this colorful handpainted porcelain that was the specialty of the Guǎngzhōu area. Foreigners clamored for this stuff. These handpainted designs incorporated both Western and Chinese themes.

11:44 A lot of Guāngcǎi was made to order specifically for importers in Europe. Gone was the simplicity and subtly of past ceramic styles. Guāngcǎi was the kind of porcelain perhaps you've all seen before that was both colorful and decorated with gold leaf. Inspired by the ceramic treasures coming out of this period in the Qing were porcelain operations in England in towns like Chelsea, Bow, Derby and perhaps most famously in Stoke-on-Trent.

12:15 Some people of substance and power back in London, after watching the global tea business grow from nothing in 1610, began to feel this business was much too big to leave in the hands of one monopolistic and increasingly unstable and unreliable trade partner, namely, China. But after all these years, still, no one had figured out how to correctly grow the tea, pick the tea and most important of all how to process the tea. Only in China did they know how to do this in the way that European people liked it.

12:54 And the Chinese guarded the process well. Tea was always grown in remote and usually mountainous areas. And because of the homogenous Han Chinese population if any non-Chinese, especially a Westerner, was seen walking around those parts, they stuck out like a sore thumb. So waltzing into the Wǔyí Mountains and poking your nose around to observe and steal all the secrets of processing tea wasn't so easy to do.

13:21 But in the first decades of the 19th century, the tea powers in the East India Company more and more felt it was bad for business to continue to be so beholden to a single supplier, China, for the entirety of their supply. When the Treaty of Nanjing was inked in 1842, there was still no place except China where quality product could be shipped in the massive quantities demanded by world markets.

13:50 And the nagging suspicion now, after humiliating the Chinese nation so badly with the Treaty of Nanjing, was that China, out of spite or economic survival, would get into the opium business themselves and that would spell the end for the EIC's opium export business. After all, if the Chinese decided to grow their own opium and supply the domestic market themselves, they could easily undercut British opium from India. And if the EIC couldn't dump the opium in China, once again they'd be stuck paying silver bullion for tea.

THE TEA HISTORY PODCAST BOOK 2
PART 15

14:24   So it became more than a feeling that something had to be done to ameliorate this disadvantageous state of affairs. When Lín Zéxú burned all the opium back in 1839, it spooked everyone. By the time of the 183's and 40s, the EIC saw China's continued tea monopoly as a clear and present danger. The tax revenues and profits generated from the tea trade were too critical to Britain. At all costs a solution was needed to break China's monopoly.

14:56   In 1830 the first tea factory was set up in Java by the Dutch to process all the tea that had been planted there in 1826. These tea seeds had come from Japan. The first Java teas to reach the markets of Amsterdam will be in 1835. If the Dutch could figure out a way, the British could too.

15:20   In the fall of 1842, with the experimental tea gardens in Assam going at full-speed, and right after the Treaty of Nanjing was signed, Robert Fortune set sail for China. He went on a botanical mission sponsored by the Royal Horticultural Society of London to research the exotic flora of China. For a young man like Fortune, 30 years old, that was quite an appointment from such an esteemed society.

15:48   Robert Fortune didn't come from money, rank or privilege. So in order to get such a plum high-profile assignment as this meant he had to be very good at his job. Fortune had worked his way up the ladder in his field the hard way. He started at the bottom, was good at what he did and thankfully he got noticed. This position as the Horticultural Society's Collector in China came

THE TEA HISTORY PODCAST BOOK 2
PART 15

thanks to the Scottish Physician and Botanist William McNabb.

16:19 If you weren't from the privileged class, signing up for something like a three-year mission to China was something people of ambition did. You never knew what could come of it and plenty of nobody's went on to make something of their lives wandering out to the hinterlands of the British Empire.

16:36 You may recall with the Treaty of Nanjing five new treaty ports had opened to direct foreign trade. The Canton System, so hated by the foreign traders, was gone at last. Now for the first time in Chinese history there were a lot of Europeans wandering around those places. So bumping into Europeans everyday wasn't common but you'd see them around. That was one thing that had changed.

17:03 The governor-general of India from 1844-1848 was Henry Hardinge. He had said of China and the tea industry, "*I deem it most desirable to afford every encouragement to the cultivation of tea in India; in my opinion the latter is likely in course of time to prove an equally prolific and more safe source of revenue to the state than now derived from the monopoly on Opium.*" Hardinge had been an early proponent of Indian tea and had even been the first to send a tin of the stuff to England.

17:39 More and more the British colonials and tea barons began to look in the direction of the Himalayas as far as where the future of the tea trade was. Indian tea had

THE TEA HISTORY PODCAST BOOK 2
PART 15

been available in Britain since the 1830s but the general consensus was that while it wasn't bad, it also wasn't quite up to snuff for the discerning British market.

18:02 Maybe you can liken this to when California wines first entered the international market. It wasn't considered respectable or as fine tasting as European wines. Nobody was flocking to buy them. The seeds for this Himalayan tea had come from China. But they weren't the best seeds and whatever they got was all they could get their hands on. They still had a long was to go. Any farmer or Monsanto executive will tell you it's all in the seeds, man. Not all *Camellia sinensis* seeds were created equal.

18:35 But despite the early dissatisfaction with the Indian tea governor-general, Hardinge hung in there as far as the potential went. Let me quote Sarah Rose from her book, "For All the Tea in China," Here she is quoting Henry Hardinge,

18:51 *"I consider it highly probable that in the course of a few years, the cultivation of Himalayan Tea is likely to prove a highly valuable source of revenue for the state. No apparent difficulties exist to the spread of tea cultivation in the Hills to an almost unlimited extent and I have every confidence that at no remote period Tea will be produced in sufficient amount not only to meet the probably large demand in India but also in quantity and sufficient fineness in quality to enable it to compete with the tea of China in European markets and to render England in some degree independent of a foreign country for its supplies of this necessity of life."*

THE TEA HISTORY PODCAST BOOK 2
PART 15

19:34 | 1843 Robert Fortune sailed into Hong Kong harbor to begin his assignment. These were the earliest days of British Hong Kong. If you recall from those History of Hong Kong episodes from the CHP, the word on the street about the colony's prospects as a trading entrepôt were mostly dismal. From Hong Kong, Fortune sailed north up the coast of China to Shanghai to the mouth of the Yangzi.

20:00 | From there, Fortune began his inaugural trip to China. He was tasked to keep his eye open for anything of horticultural value and to bring back as many specimens as possible for further study in London. He was told to also look for anything of value concerning tea.

20:20 | He found a lot of things out but perhaps most important of all was the knowledge that green tea and black tea both came from the same exact plant. If I may, I wanted to take a few quotes from Robert Fortune's book titled, "Three Years Wanderings in The Northern Provinces of China." Now, he didn't really wander north of Shanghai so technically his wanderings weren't in the Northern Provinces. But he did get around Zhejiang, Jiangsu and Fujian and that counted for something.

20:51 | This book written by Fortune was published after his return to England in 1849. This trip made him. Being quite a trained and disciplined botanist and horticulturist himself, the observations and notations Fortune made were astounding. The book and his whole adventure in China were a sensation in their day.

THE TEA HISTORY PODCAST BOOK 2
PART 15

21:14 Let me quote from Fortune's book,

21:16 *"There are few subjects connected with the vegetable kingdom which have attracted such a large share of public notice as the tea-plant of China. Its cultivation on the Chinese hills, the particular species or variety which produced the black and green teas of commerce, and the method of preparing the leaves, have always been objects of peculiar interest. The jealousy of the Chinese government, in former times, prevented foreigners from visiting any of the districts where tea is cultivated. And hence we find English authors contradicting each other, some asserting that the black and green teas are produced by the same variety, and that the difference in color is the result of a different mode of preparation, while others say that the black teas are produced from the plant called by botanists Thea Bohea, and the green from Thea veridis, both of which we have had for many years in our gardens in England."*

22:12 Fortune had seen first-hand that *"the greater part of the black and green teas which are brought yearly from China to Europe and America are obtained from the same species or variety, namely from the Thea veridis. Great was my surprise to find all the plants on the tea hills near Fuzhou exactly the same as those in the green tea districts of the north. Although the specific differences of the tea-plants were well known to me, I was so much surprised, and I may add amused, at this discovery, that I procured a set of specimens for the herbarium, and also dug up a living plant, which I took northward to Zhejiang. On comparing it with those which grow on the green tea hills, no difference whatsoever was observed."*

THE TEA HISTORY PODCAST BOOK 2
PART 15

23:01 And with that, the great Swede Karl Linnaeus himself was proven wrong by Fortune regarding black and green tea coming from two different species of tea plant. Fortune made some interesting observations during his China journey. This book can be obtained online for free. I downloaded a pdf version.

23:21 Fortune said of the first teas of the season to be picked:

23:26 *"In the green tea districts of Zhejiang near Ningbo, the first crop of leaves is generally gathered around the middle of April. This consists of the young leaf-buds just as they begin to unfold, and forms a fine and delicate kind of young hyson, which is held in high estimation by the natives, and is generally sent about in small quantities as presents to their friends. It is a scarce and expensive article, and the picking of the leaves in such a young state does considerable injury to the tea plantations. The summer rains, however, which fall copiously about this season, moisten the earth and air, and if the plants are young and vigorous they soon push out fresh leaves."*

24:13 It's said that on this adventurous three-year trip Fortune acquired enough of a proficiency in Mandarin so that if he dressed up in a Chinese official's garb, if nobody got too close, he could pass for a local.

24:26 And I don't want to leave you hanging or anything, but I'm going to leave you hanging until next time when we pick up with Episode 16 to discuss the real star of this whole enterprise, the one who made Fortune's success

THE TEA HISTORY PODCAST BOOK 2
PART 15

in China all possible with his revolutionary but simple invention. It helped change the world. You won't want to miss that, so do consider coming back for more.

24:51 That's a gonna be it for me this time. Laszlo Montgomery signing off from the city of Los Angeles in Der goldene Staat. I'm really hoping to see you next time for another episodio delicioso of the Tea History Podcast.

The Tea History Podcast
Book 2 Part 16

THE TRANSCRIPTS

SUMMARY

The hero who made Robert Fortune's success assured, Dr. Nathanial Bagshaw Ward, is introduced in this episode. Ward's invention of the terrarium was the one thing that ensured Fortune's hard work in China wouldn't be wasted. We see how Fortune went into China, scored plants and tea seeds from Zhejiang, Anhui and Fujian and got everything safely transported to India.

TRANSCRIPT

00:00 Welcome back everyone. Laszlo Montgomery with you once again. Part 16 this time. We ended so abruptly last episode and I left you hanging somewhat, making you wait for me to reveal the true superstar of this whole adventure, someone who not only ensured the success of Robert Fortune's trip but had no small impact on the world of botany, horticulture and a whole lot more.

00:24 The real star of this mission wasn't so much Fortune as much as it was Dr. Nathaniel Bagshaw Ward, 1791-1868. In the 1830s Ward invented an air-tight glass and wood case that could be used to transport plant species that grew in almost any climate, over long distances. Basically, this device is what we know as a terrarium.

THE TEA HISTORY PODCAST BOOK 2
PART 16

00:52 In 1829 Ward placed some soil and dried leaves into a sealed glass bottle. He also inserted the pupa of a sphinx moth. He did this with the intention to observe the moth emerge from the cocoon.

01:07 But unexpectedly he observed a fern and some meadow grass beginning to sprout from the soil. This accidental discovery led Ward to conclude that plants enclosed in sealed glass containers could survive for long periods without watering.

01:27 He continued his experiments for the next four years and with this knowledge he went on to design these sturdy glazed cases that would be able to transport plant specimens from one end of the world to the other.

01:42 By 1833, his invention had successfully shipped plant specimens from London to Sydney. Ever since the dawn of the Age of Exploration, these adventurers tried like crazy to bring back to their lands all these flora specimens they found overseas. But all that salty air on the voyage back killed everything.

02:06 In 1842, Ward published a book, "On the Growth of Plants in Closely Glazed Cases" which laid out how this all worked and why. And he never patented it or tried to get rich off of his discovery. He just shared this incredible new technology with whoever wanted it. The British East India Company of course took a great interest in this book. I bet they would have patented it.

THE TEA HISTORY PODCAST BOOK 2
PART 16

02:32 Up to Robert Fortune's time, whenever plant hunters brought cuttings and samples back to the home country, most everything died on the way. With these Wardian Cases as they were called, as long as you didn't break the seal and kept the interior environment the same as when you first sealed it, the plant inside would keep growing and thriving.

02:55 This meant that now, the risk of hauling live tea plants from China to India or for that matter, to London, would be no big deal. With this knowledge and with the help of these Wardian Cases Fortune had been able to haul back a nice bounty of specimens to the Royal Horticultural Society.

03:16 So let's get back to Fortune's adventures. From his book of his travels, "Three Years Wanderings in The Northern Provinces of China" he had this to say about the secrets to turning freshly picked tea leaves into the finished product, Fortune wrote,

03:32 *"The mode of gathering and preparing the leaves of the tea-plants is extremely simple. We have so long accustomed to magnify and mystify every thing relating to the Chinese, that in all their arts and manufactures, we expect to find some peculiar and out of the way practice, when the fact is, that many operations in China are more simple in their character than in most other parts of the world. To rightly understand the process of rolling and drying the leaves, which I am about to describe, it must be borne in mind that the grand object is to expel the moisture, and at*

THE TEA HISTORY PODCAST BOOK 2
PART 16

>the same time to retain, as much as possible, of the aromatic and other desirable secretions of the species. The system adopted to attain this end is as simple as it is efficacious."

04:25 This book that Fortune wrote about all his wanderings around this time 1843-1844-1845 really is great reading.

04:36 From this initial sojourn to China, Fortune brought back invaluable information that was used to make advances not only in botany but in commerce as well.

04:47 These chaps like Robert Fortune were the real Indiana Jones's of their day. They went out into the wild, mixed with the natives, risked their lives and carried out these amazing adventures all for the sake of science or some noble cause.

05:05 In his book, Fortune describes all manners of close calls that he had along the way, any one of them big enough to scuttle the whole operation. But despite all the hardships, he managed to survive. As far as disguising his appearance wherever he went Fortune wrote,

05:24 > "I was, of course, traveling in the Chinese costume; my head was shaved, I had a splendid wig and tail, of which some Chinaman in former days had doubtless been extremely vain, and upon the whole I believe I made a pretty fair Chinaman. Although the Chinese countenance and eyes differ considerably from those of a native of Europe, yet a traveller in the north has a far greater chance of escaping detection than in the

THE TEA HISTORY PODCAST BOOK 2
PART 16

> *south of China, the features of the northern natives approaching more nearly to those of Europeans than they do in the south, and the difference amongst themselves also being greater."*

06:01 Fortune got to see first hand how tea was made. The withering. The firing. The drying, everything. He took meticulous notes and made drawings of every step of the process.

06:15 Many of the most popular teas of the world achieve their maximum greatness through the rolling process. This is what gives different kinds of teas their unique appearance and shape, not to mention, taste as well. Here Fortune described what he observed,

06:34 > *"A quantity of leaves, from a sieve or basket, are now thrown into the pans, and turned over, shaken up, and kept in motion by men and women stationed there for this purpose. The leaves are immediately affected by the heat. They begin to crack, and become quite moist with the vapor or sap which they give out on the application of heat. This part of the process lasts about five minutes, in which time the leaves lose their crispness, and become soft and pliable. They are then taken out of the pans and thrown upon a table, the upper part of which is made of split pieces of bamboo. Three or four persons now surround the table, and the heap of tea leaves is divided into as many parcels, each individual taking as many as he can hold in his hands, and the rolling process commences. I cannot give a better idea of this operation than by comparing it to a*

THE TEA HISTORY PODCAST BOOK 2
PART 16

baker working and rolling his dough. Both hands are used in the very same way; the object being to express the sap and moisture, and at the same time to twist the leaves. The leaves being pressed, twisted and curled, do not occupy a quarter of the space which they did before the operation."

07:54 When Fortune was finishing up this first stint in China, he had spent time in Canton and wrote an entire chapter in his book about all the teas for sale there that ended up in Western markets. He mentions all the names you've heard throughout this series. Bohea, Congou, Souchong, Pekoe, Hyson, Young Hyson and Gunpowder.

08:17 Fortune arrived back in England three years after he left. He brought many of the more than two hundred new species of plants he would discover during his illustrious career. In his final remarks in his book he had written:

08:31 "When we arrived at Hong Kong, I divided my collections, and dispatched eight glazed cases of the living plants for England: the duplicates of these and many others I reserved to take under my own care. I went up to Canton and took my passage for London in the ship 'John Cooper'. Eighteen glazed cases, filled with the most beautiful plants of northern China, were placed upon the poop of the ship, and we sailed on the 22nd of December. After a long but favorable voyage we anchored in the Thames, on the 6th of May, 1846. The plants arrived in excellent order, and were immediately conveyed to the garden of the Horticultural Society

THE TEA HISTORY PODCAST BOOK 2
PART 16

> at Chiswick. Already, many of those which I first imported have found their way to the principal gardens in Europe; and at the present time (October 20, 1846), the Anemone japonica is in full bloom in the garden of the Society at Chiswick, as luxuriant and beautiful as it ever grew on the graves of the Chinese, near the ramparts of Shanghai."

09:40 So with the proven success of utilizing Ward's cases, the high-ups in the East India Company inner circle knew that the wherewithal finally existed to safely and successfully get the tea seeds and live plants out of China and shipped to an Indian port. From the Indian port the cases would then have to be schlepped in one piece high up to the Himalayas to the experimental tea gardens at Saharanpur and ultimately to Assam and Darjeeling.

10:13 By the 1840's early efforts to successfully grow tea in the Himalayas were coming along quite nicely. The EIC now had the confidence to carry out by our modern definition, a kind of corporate espionage. To quote from Sarah Rose's book "For all the Tea in China", "Tea met all the definitions of intellectual property: it was a product of high commercial value, it was manufactured using a formula and process unique to China, which China protected fiercely; and it gave China a vast advantage over its competitors."

10:52 So the EIC went to Robert Fortune, still basking in the afterglow of his successful China operation. In order to entice him into taking on this mission impossible, they offered to pay him five times his current salary

THE TEA HISTORY PODCAST BOOK 2
PART 16

plus transport to and from China. They approved all his reasonable expenses. And best of all as far as Robert Fortune was concerned, anything else that he picked up along the way as far as new species of plants, including the seeds, belonged to him.

11:26 All the Honorable Company wanted out of him were live tea plants and enough tea seeds to kick start the whole Indian tea operation. If they were going to scale this tea venture in India they were going to need a lot of seeds, over a hundred thousand if they could get their hands on that much.

11:44 Another part of the EIC's plan involved procuring trained tea masters from China to come to India to consult to the British and Indian planters based there. They were hot for all the fine points to growing and processing the tea. And not only the tea experts were required, Fortune was told to bring back any and all tools and implements used in the manufacturing of tea.

12:10 Up to this point Governor-General Hardinge had 600 acres of local tea under cultivation in India that, as I said, showed promise but wasn't exportable quality yet. A lot of that was due to the software. They had the tea bushes, which was a start. These were the Assam varietal of the *Camellia sinensis* tea bush. Remember from Tea Part 1 you have the China, Assam and Java varietals of the *Camellia sinensis* tea plant.

12:42 So when 1848 rolled around, Fortune was successfully recruited by the EIC to go in and do their dirty work.

THE TEA HISTORY PODCAST BOOK 2
PART 16

12:51 | Sarah Rose quoted the EIC's instructions sent by letter to Fortune:

12:57 | *"Besides the collection of tea plants and seeds from the best localities for transmission to India, it will be your duty to avail yourself of every opportunity of acquiring information as to the cultivation of the tea plant and the manufacture of tea as practiced by the Chinese and on all other points with which it may be desirable that those entrusted with the superintendence of the tea nurseries in India should be made acquainted."*

13:25 | Fortune very strongly believed tea was a substance so important to humankind that it shouldn't be controlled by a single supplier. He went to his grave believing he didn't do anything wrong.

13:38 | So Fortune's mission impossible, should he decide to accept it, was to get as many live plants as possible out of China along with a huge quantity of seeds. Just like that. And while he was at it, he also had to procure sufficient tea masters, to bring all those brain cells to India and show everybody how they turned all those freshly picked leaves into that magical cuppa that only they knew how to do. Everyone has their price, I guess. And procuring the experts to teach the secrets ended up not being that difficult at all.

14:16 | By the fall of 1848, Robert Fortune was dressed up like a 1940s Hollywood movie star Yellow-facing a Chinese person. Just like last time he was in China. If anyone got too close there was a chance they might mistake him for

THE TEA HISTORY PODCAST BOOK 2
PART 16

a foreigner wearing a Chinese getup. So he had to be as low-key and aloof as possible.

14:36 Together with his A-team of servants and his trusty guide, a local from the Wǔyí Mountain area, he took off first in the direction of Zhèjiāng and Ānhuī. The Wǔyí Mountains would follow. He already knew Zhèjiāng and the Huángshān area of Ānhuī was where the Chinese grew all their best green teas. So, getting the lowdown about everything there was to know about green tea was his immediate mission.

15:03 Last trip, Fortune produced a treasure trove of new understanding. Now he was filling in all the missing info. He learned quickly about the withering process that was so critical to green tea. He noted that as soon as the tea leaves were plucked they were taken to a central location and spread out over these large rattan plates and allowed to dry anywhere from one to two hours.

15:30 Fortune vividly noted everything he observed as the raw material was passed from process to process. Since green tea involved the least amount of processing, this was easier than when he was trying to figure out the black tea process.

15:46 He watched as the slightly withered leaves were next taken to a kind of furnace room where batches of withered leaves were put into a kind of wok heated to just the right temperature. No thermostats back then and they were still using wood fires. The tea master mixing the leaves in that heated wok had to maintain that fire so as to heat the wok to the optimum setting possible. No manuals were written about how to do this. It was something passed down from parents to children and in time you just knew how to do it perfectly.

16:23 If you're interested, you can see how they do this in any number of Yōukù and YouTube videos. I think there are multiple videos of tea makers making every kind of tea. As they work their magic, you can hear the leaves sizzle and crackle slightly as the moist part of the leaf comes to the surface. That's where all the flavor was. By the end of this step, the tea leaf will have been reduced to about 25% of its original size.

16:52 Next step was the rolling part. There were so many different ways to do this. How the loose leaf tea appears when you open up that air-tight package is determined mostly by this process. Some tea leaves are extremely small, composed of buds only. How each particular village rolls their tea after the first firing is always unique to them. Gunpowder tea, for example, gets rolled into these little pellets. Lóng Jǐng Dragon Well tea leaves are pressed flat. All teas have their distinct look.

17:33 Fortune also wrote about the tedious sorting process, how the leaves are separated into grades. I actually saw this process with my own eyes when I was out in Qióngláі, Sichuan Province. I observed a bunch of workers all sitting around a table filled with heaps of finished tea. They spent all day there, nimble fingers separating the stems from the broken leaves from the

THE TEA HISTORY PODCAST BOOK 2
PART 16

unbroken leaves. The unbroken leaves as you might imagine cost the most and were the most prized.

18:07 If you break open your mass market tea bag you'll see there aren't any unbroken leaves in there. What you have is called CTC tea. CTC means Crush-Tear-Curl. This process was developed in the 1930s and within a few decades was the standard mass production method of producing tea destined for tea bags.

18:31 When the dried leaf is processed this way it produces a nice quick brew of dark tea. Almost all the tea in India, more than 80%, ends up as CTC tea. The experts and tea snobs wouldn't be caught dead drinking this stuff. Not all tea bags use CTC tea. You can get high-end loose leaf tea now in these pyramid shaped and extra sized tea bags designed for whole leaf artisanal teas.

19:03 Robert Fortune made the rounds and recorded all his observations. I'll tell you, both the Royal Horticultural Society the first time around and now the East India Company sure picked the right person for the job. Not only was Fortune a first rate botanist and all-around man of science, he was an incredible adventurer as well. Every expat living in China today surely can appreciate how rough going it must have been for a foreigner to get around there in the late 1840s compared to today. He faced a lot of hardships and had plenty of close calls. But Fortune was able to roll with every punch thrown at him.

THE TEA HISTORY PODCAST BOOK 2
PART 16

19:45 | I have to say this was quite a con job he did. I can hardly think of anything more conspicuous than the spectacle it must have been carrying all those Ward cases and supplies through the mountains and villages. And I'm sure some were fooled by Fortune's costume, but I'm betting most of the villagers saw something that wasn't quite right about that very strange looking Chinese guy in the sedan chair.

20:12 | On this second visit to China, Robert Fortune stumbled onto something that later on is going to provide a number of nails that will close the coffin on China's tea export business to Europe. In his trek around Ānhuī and Zhejiang, especially around Hangzhou, he noted with some horror that during one of the final processes, the Chinese workers were adding some sort of blue-green pigment to the tea to give it a particular coloring.

20:42 | Let me quote what Fortune said about this in his later work, "The Tea Districts of China and India." He said,

20:49 | *"Having procured a portion of Prussian-blue, he threw it into a porcelain bowl, not unlike a chemists mortar, and crushed it into a very fine powder. At the same time a quantity of gypsum was produced and burned in the charcoal first which were then roasting the teas, The object of this was to soften it, in order that it might be readily pounded into a very fine powder, in the same manner as the Prussian-blue had been. The gypsum, having been taken out of the fire after a certain time had elapsed, readily crumbled down and was reduced to a powder in the mortar. These two substances, having*

THE TEA HISTORY PODCAST BOOK 2
PART 16

been thus prepared were then mixed together in the proportion of four parts of gypsum to three parts of Prussian-blue and formed a light blue powder, which was then ready for use. This coloring matter was applied to the teas during the process of roasting."

21:46 Ain't that something. Incredible that Fortune stumbled on this. Prussian-blue, if you never heard of it before, is a pigment that's derived from hydrogen cyanide if that gives you any hint about whether or not it should be used as an additive in the tea manufacturing process. Fortune also wrote,

22:06 "One day an English gentleman in Shanghai being in conversation with some Chinese from the green-tea country, asked them what reason they had for dyeing the tea and whether it would not be better without undergoing the process. They justly remarked that as foreigners seemed to prefer having a mixture of Prussian-blue and gypsum with their tea to make it look uniform and pretty, and as these ingredients were cheap enough, the Chinese had no objection to supply them, especially as such teas always fetched a higher price."

22:38 Doing a little arithmetic, Fortune had been able to figure out that the typical green tea drinker in the Americas or in England had by this time consumed about half a pound each of Prussian-blue and gypsum. Wait till that word gets out.

THE TEA HISTORY PODCAST BOOK 2
PART 16

22:56 | The next stop for Fortune was to Wǔyí Shan, arguably China's most celebrated area for tea. There he enjoyed the convenience of shacking up at his aide's residence. I'm not saying much about this local guide, surnamed Wang. But he was quite an interesting and conniving soul. Sarah Rose gives some nice descriptions about this Mr. Wang. He was a tea producer himself, local to northern Fujian and was invaluable to Robert Fortune as a fixer for everything he needed.

23:29 | Fortune set up his operation at Wang's residence and began at once gathering plants and seeds. This was supposed to be a three-week operation at most in the Wǔyí Mountains.

23:41 | Let me quote Fortune as he beheld the splendor of the Wǔyí Mountains,

23:46 | *"For some times past I had been, as it were, amongst a sea of mountains, but now the famed Bohea ranges lay before me in all their grandeur, with their tops piercing through the lower clouds, and showing themselves far above them. They seemed to be broken up into thousands of fragments, some of which had the most remarkable and striking outlines."*

24:14 | Fortune observed an army of tea pickers, all women, who worked these tea gardens scattered all over the Wǔyí mountain area. They worked sunup to sundown April through October.

THE TEA HISTORY PODCAST BOOK 2
PART 16

24:27 Each tea bush would be picked over every ten days. Only the tea leaves from the tips were plucked. A good picker, he noted, could pick thirty-thousand tea shoots a day. Approximately thirty-two hundred shoots equaled a pound. That amounted to about ten pounds a day per picker. At a four or five to one ratio of fresh leaves to fully processed, that wasn't a lot of tea per picker. That's why you had to have a lot of them. *Ren duo hao ban shi.* Chairman Mao once said that, and he sure was right in this instance. The more people you have doing the job, the easier it is to get things done.

25:07 This was one of those things the Chinese had figured out over the centuries. That by aggressively picking the leaves every ten days like they did, it caused the bush, as a self-defense mechanism, to ooze more sap into the leaves.

25:22 There were temples scattered everywhere throughout the Wǔyí Mountains and the monks who called the temple home were all actively involved in the growing and processing of tea. After spending enough time watching everything up close and gathering all the plants and seeds, Fortune had what he had come to collect.

25:42 He had this final observation to make about tea.

25:46 *"It is an exceedingly useful plant; cultivate it, and the benefit will be widely spread, drink it, and the animal spirits will be lively and clear. The chief rulers, dukes, and nobility esteem it; the lower people, the poor and the beggarly, will not be destitute of it; all use it daily, and like it... Drinking it tends to clear away all impurities, drives off drowsiness, removes or prevents headaches, and it is universally in high esteem."*

26:20 By January 1849, Fortune was pleased to inform the head office that, "I have much pleasure in informing you that I have procured a large supply of seeds and young plants which I trust will get safely to India. These were procured in different parts of the country, some from a celebrated tea farm."

26:40 Next episode we're going to pick up at the point when this tea procured by Fortune on this trip is transported to India. Believe it or not, Fortune's part of this black op was mostly finished. But there was still a whole heck of a lot more to do before they'd be packaging tea up in the Indian Himalayas and shipping it to Europe. Everyone involved in this risky endeavor still had a very long and winding road to hoe before the champagne corks could be popped. But Fortune, at least, had done his part.

27:15 Everything, the seeds, the seedlings, plant cuttings, all were packed inside the airtight Ward cases and readied for transport. Once everything was laden on board a cargo vessel in Shanghai, there was still a rather long and uncertain voyage to Calcutta. This is still the mid 19th century and these kinds of voyages were still fraught with all kinds of dangers that still happened regularly on the high seas.

 THE TEA HISTORY PODCAST BOOK 2
PART 16

27:45 | Once the vessel arrived in India there was still the logistical headache of getting everything from the plains of Calcutta to the foothills of the Himalayas. This was very fragile cargo packed inside even more fragile glass cases. We'll look at how all this played out next episode. They had some close calls.

28:06 | So in Part 17, we'll pick up where we left off and what the profound aftereffects were on the British tea trade with China. The idea had all along been to steal the secrets of tea from China and use this stolen knowledge to build a new tea industry from the ground up in lands where the British were in the driver's seat. Then, as far as the EIC was concerned China could be as capricious, uncooperative and arbitrary as they wanted. If Robert Fortune and everyone else involved in this operation did their job well, no one would need Chinese tea anymore.

28:44 | You know, in the 1870's the British were able to secret out of Brazil, seeds for the indigenous rubber trees. And they packed them in these Wardian Cases and took them to Sri Lanka and their thriving enterprise they had going on in Malaya and kickstarted the whole rubber industry there.

29:03 | Anyway, more Robert Fortune next time. I hope you'll come back and see how this all pans out.

29:09 | So until that time, may it not be too long, this is Laszlo Montgomery signing off from sunny Los Angeles here in the State of Confusion.

THE TEA HISTORY PODCAST BOOK 2
PART 16

29:20 I hope you enjoyed today's episode and that you'll maybe consider joining me next time for another fine tasting episode of the Tea History Podcast.

The Tea History Podcast
Book 2 Part 17

SUMMARY

After enjoying a monopoly that lasted for 45 centuries, China's secrets of how they turned *Camellia sinensis* leaves into tea are shared with the world (but not by the Chinese). This time we see how the tea seeds, plants, tools, and experts are secreted out of China and successfully transported to the Indian highlands. There a British dream team of botanists and horticulturalists take over the job begun by Robert Fortune and launch the tea industry in India. We also look at James Taylor's efforts to plant tea in Ceylon and how his business savvy partner in this venture brought tea to the world. This partner was Thomas J. Lipton, the one who brought us the ubiquitous Lipton Tea. What a character he was!

TRANSCRIPT

00:00	Hey everyone, how's it going? Laszlo Montgomery here starting to wind things down on this epic history of Tea overview. Part 17 today.
00:09	Oh man! China had such a good run. 2737 BCE all the way to 1850. 4,587 years. That's a nice stretch by anyone's reckoning. Shoot, Standard Oil only had their monopoly for, not even forty years.
00:29	It's really amazing that with tea growing in many other places besides China, after so long no one except the Chinese had figured out how to turn those leaves into

THE TEA HISTORY PODCAST BOOK 2
PART 17

teas that were so tasty they inspired a million poems, paintings and countless literary and artistic works, not to mention probably no small amount of witty and interesting conversation.

00:54 The Koreans and Japanese of course had their great contributions to tea culture, but it's pretty well known from whom they originally drew their earliest inspiration.

01:06 In the last episode, I introduced Mr. Robert Fortune, a botanist who lived a very charmed and adventurous life. He had taken on this very dangerous and life-threatening assignment from the East India Company that, as I said, amounted to international espionage.

01:24 Now Lew, over in New York City, my longtime China History Podcast listener, supporter and tea connoisseur extraordinaire as well as the proprietor of the wonderful tea resource Babelcarp.org, the Tea Lexicon and probably many others besides, believes Robert Fortune didn't commit industrial espionage as much as he acted as a 19th century open source pioneer. That's for all ya'lls to decide. There are multiple ways to look at what Robert Fortune did on his first two China trips.

01:59 We left off last time in Part 16 with Fortune halfway home before he could breathe easy and say the magic words: Mission Accomplished. Since the ultimate objective was to transplant all the goodness of Chinese tea into Indian soil, getting everything on board the vessel at the China port was only half the battle. They still had to get all the seeds, seedlings and saplings to their final destination, alive, across the waves in the dead of winter and up into the mountains. For this voyage, packed onboard were 13,000 young plants and five gallons of seeds.

02:40 The contents were divided up amongst four vessels. In this way, if one or two ships went down to Davy Jones' Locker, there were still backups. Fortune only went as far as Hong Kong. Once again, the Wardian Cases invented, tested and proven effective in the field by Fortune were the unsung heroes of that momentous 19th century saga. Dr. Nathaniel Bagshaw Ward. Quite an impact on the world he ended up having with his invention of the terrarium. This invention, by the way, led to the vivarium and the aquarium.

03:15 Fortune had managed to pick a first-rate crew of gardeners to babysit everything and ensure the integrity of the cases from port to port. One had to be very careful because, once you opened up the Wardian Case or a crack appeared, it was over for the contents. When you sealed it shut, the whole system inside the Ward Case maintained itself.

03:38 Fortune had done his job well for the company. Now it was time for him to kick back and let his counterparts in India take over the operation. If Fortune was the perfect man for the undercover job in China, Hugh Falconer was the best man for all that needed to be followed up in India. He was a Scotsman like Fortune who already enjoyed some fame and repute as an accomplished paleontologist, geologist and botanist.

THE TEA HISTORY PODCAST BOOK 2
PART 17

04:07 | Falconer had already been in the tea business in India since 1834. He had been chosen by the British officials in that part of India to spearhead the development of tea plantations in India that could compete with, and later supplant, all Chinese tea imports. He had left India for many years but found himself back in the employ of the government managing the tea operation that Fortune was participating in. His role was to be on the receiving end of the cargo and to manage the transport of the China tea to its first destination, the Saharanpur Experimental Gardens in Uttar Pradesh. That was a good 1,500 kilometers from the Mountains of Assam to the east.

04:53 | As the tea made its way up the mountains to its final destination a bit of a disaster occurred when some dimwit official went and opened up the Wardian cases to take a look inside. But whatever calamity like this, big or small that the group encountered as they made their way to Saharanpur, they got through it by improvising.

05:14 | Once they arrived at the Experimental Gardens station, they were met by Deputy Surgeon General William Jameson. He was serving in his early years of a long stint at the garden that would last till 1875.

05:30 | Of the 13,000 seedlings of green tea bush, a thousand were still alive but by the time they reached their destination only 3% of what left China was still viable. So although everything made it on board the vessel okay, in the end they learned from this green tea mission

THE TEA HISTORY PODCAST BOOK 2
PART 17

that the transport methods were equally as important as the procurement.

05:54 In retrospect, Jameson ended up being the weak link in the chain of key players. Falconer blamed the failure of the mission on Jameson, and Jameson pointed his finger at Falconer. It was a huge disappointment and somewhat of a setback. Fortune had gone to a lot of trouble in Anhui and Zhejiang to procure these seeds and plants.

06:16 Bear in mind when this was happening. In 1850 all the tea developed in India had been green tea. Black tea is still not quite yet a reality in India. So getting that black tea process just right was important to the tea planters in India working in the employ of the British authorities.

06:39 What was happening now in the northeast of India was sure going to be important down the line to the people in the sugar business in the West Indies. Their product was destined to sweeten the tea in dozens of millions of teacups the world over.

06:56 The scandal of the Prussian blue and gypsum being added to green tea as food coloring caused a seismic shift in the popular demand for an alternative brew. The first world's fair, the 1851 Great Exhibition, held in Crystal Palace, turned out to be the perfect venue to announce the matter of these toxic additives being maliciously mixed in with China green tea.

07:22 With the introduction of this deadly food scandal into the public discourse it had predictable results. It caused

THE TEA HISTORY PODCAST BOOK 2
PART 17

the British public to more quickly accept this new Indian black tea over the Chinese tea they had known all their lives. Black tea was standing in the wings when green tea got that bad rap. And when China tea got a bad name, the Indian tea industry was just getting ready to stand up for the first time.

07:50 Fortune received word about the setback in the green tea mission while he was still in China. Now this black tea mission with its goal to procure the best specimens he could get his hands on in the Wǔyí Mountain area was gonna be even more important. A newer and more reliable transport method had to be figured out.

08:12 Fortune did things different this time around when it came time to ship this new lot of tea. He came up with this brilliant idea to ship the seeds already planted in the soil inside the Wardian Cases. This turned out to be the game-changing simple solution to the vexing problem.

08:35 By the time this vessel arrived in Calcutta the tea seeds packed in the four foot by six foot glass cases had all germinated. That is to say, of the 20,000 China tea seedlings packed by Fortune, 12,838 had survived the trip, sprouted, and were beginning to grow. Fortune tried this transport method again, sending another shipment of planted seeds. Everything arrived in perfect shape. This new method thought up by Fortune was not only more effective than shipping actual plants, it was also much easier to execute.

09:20 Now they had to get them into the Indian soil and

THE TEA HISTORY PODCAST BOOK 2
PART 17

launch a multi-billion dollar industry. To do this, Fortune used his relationship with the traders Dent & Co. to procure the employment services of eight China tea experts. These eight Chinese signed a three-year deal to stay in India and show the plantation workers and management everything there was to know about how they did it back in Fujian. Quoting from Sarah Rose's Book, "For all the Tea in China" again, the contract these eight men signed went like this,

09:54 "*I, whoever, a Chinese Tea maker, hereby engage to proceed to the Himalayan Gardens to manufacture tea in the Government Tea plantations on a monthly salary of fifteen dollars or thirty-three Rupees commencing from such and such a date and I bind myself to serve for a period of three years. I further engage that I will work diligently as a tea cultivator or in any other manner in which I can be useful and failing any part of the engagement I shall be liable to pay a fine of one hundred dollars to my employers. I acknowledge having received from Mr. Fortune on the part of the government an advance of two months wages or thirty dollars.*"

10:36 They left Shanghai in 1851 and sailed the route that took them to India.

10:42 Fortune risked his life to steal the tea seeds and plants and he managed to walk out of eastern China with the processing technology as well. And as if this weren't enough, he also figured out how to safely and successfully transport the fragile cargo. Then for his encore, Robert Fortune managed to rustle up eight tea

 THE TEA HISTORY PODCAST BOOK 2
PART 17

experts from China who were willing to sell out their country for a pittance by transferring this technology to the British in India. And last I checked, the British or Indian government never sent any royalty checks to Beijing.

11:18　When the Chinese tea experts arrived at the location in northern India they brought, in addition to the knowledge stored in their brains, all the necessary equipment to process the tea: ovens, woks and cultivation tools. There they bred and cross-bred all the seeds and plants that Fortune brought from China with the local Indian tea plants. Then through the next several generations, utilizing all the selective breeding techniques learned over time, they gradually got it all right. Gregor Mendel was laying the groundwork for modern genetics right around this time, mid to late 1860s. It was a very exciting time in plant genetics.

12:02　The great minds working on this mini-Manhattan Project figured it all out and were able to take full advantage of the topography, climate and soil of the Bengal region. Into the 1850s and 1860s, the combined efforts of everyone involved got it all up and running.

12:22　Today in 2021... of the four billion or so kilos of tea production in the world, India now produces a quarter of that. Though China is the largest exporter of tea at 2.4 million metric tonnes of tea, Assam state in India today is the largest single tea-growing region in the whole world. Around the world, over three billion cups a day of tea are consumed.

THE TEA HISTORY PODCAST BOOK 2
PART 17

12:56 | Fresh on the heels of their success in Assam, another new tea town was planned in Darjeeling, seven thousand feet above sea level. The Darjeeling operation was seeded with tea seedlings developed at the experimental station still going strong in Saharanpur. The man in charge in Darjeeling was Archibald Campbell. Campbell, as an experiment, had early on planted seeds in Darjeeling that showed a great deal of promise. This is what led him to higher-ups in authority who took an interest in his early results.

13:28 | In March 1851, Fortune arrived in India to finally see first-hand what was going on with the tea enterprise that he would later be called the father of. He went to Saharanpur first and saw a thriving operation. He got on famously with Campbell who would be credited together with Fortune for the unparalleled success of the operation. Everything Fortune brought back was carefully planted. Even eighty per cent of the plants considered beyond saving that came from the first green tea shipment made a miraculous recovery. Despite the hardships and missteps along the way, this operation was by all accounts a great achievement both scientifically and commercially.

14:14 | Seeds originally brought back from the Wǔyí Mountain area were planted in Darjeeling and this formed the earliest base stock of Darjeeling tea. The earliest plants experimented on by Campbell had not worked as well and the flavors were not quite up to par. But in a single generation after planting the tea seeds Fortune brought from Fujian province, the Indian tea industry had grown

THE TEA HISTORY PODCAST BOOK 2
PART 17

from a seed to become, next to China, the world leader in production volume, exports, and in pricing as well. And not only that, in the European and American markets, the Indian tea soon bested the competitive product from China. And although this was a subjective matter, the tea tasters working for the British firms considered the black tea from India to be superior in taste as well.

15:07 Today, Darjeeling tea is called the champagne of teas. Darjeeling is famous for black tea, but you'll see in recent years growers in West Bengal are also giving the Chinese a run for their money with their green, white and oolong teas. Darjeeling tea, although it's called a black tea, is technically an oolong because the oxidation of the leaf isn't 100% like in other blacks.

15:33 After China lost all that export business, they never got it back. In 1879 over 70% of the tea sold in England still came from China. By 1900, this share was down to 10% and falling.

15:52 The way global demand for tea had grown in the mid to late 1800s, it had become too overwhelming for China's supply chain. China's tea manufacturing industry, as big as it was, was very fragmented, supplied by an intricate network of small-time operations run by temples, individual tea farmers and families. It was terribly inefficient for the kind of demand that needed to be ramped up to satisfy the rapidly growing 19th century global markets.

THE TEA HISTORY PODCAST BOOK 2
PART 17

16:23 | The way the British set everything up in India, the whole operation was geared towards the most efficient mass production methods possible. They only produced black tea. That was it.

16:38 | I didn't mention Sri Lanka yet because that's a whole other fantastic story regarding their tea industry there. Let me just touch on Sri Lanka or Ceylon as it was called back in the day. Not many people know this, but it was James Taylor who launched the whole tea industry there. Not Sweet Baby James. A different James Taylor, another Scotsman of course. He arrived in Ceylon in 1852 and worked with yet another Scotsman, though of Irish parentage, who I'm sure you all heard of: Thomas Johnstone Lipton of the Lipton Tea Company.

17:16 | Lipton started his business in Scotland, in Glasgow. He started with one shop selling hams, sides of bacon, eggs, you know one of these kinds of old-time stores. That first shop located on Stobcross Street in Glasgow led to several more, and before long, his Lipton Markets were found in England and Ireland as well.

17:40 | In 1889 when Thomas J. Lipton got into the tea business, he imported 20,000 chests of tea. And the P.T. Barnum in Thomas Lipton created this public spectacle when the tea arrived at port. He hired a brass band that paraded the tea through the streets of Glasgow. Lipton's company grabbed their initial chunk of market share by aggressively undercutting the competition on price.

 THE TEA HISTORY PODCAST BOOK 2
PART 17

18:07 | From May to October 1893, the World's Columbian Exposition, a.k.a. the Chicago World's Fair, was held. Good thing they didn't hold it in the winter. The Fair was held on 630 acres in what is today the Jackson Park, Midway, Hyde Park and Woodlawn neighborhoods of Chicago, where my parents grew up. 27 million people walked through the grounds. And it was at this venue, the Chicago World's Fair of 1893 that Lipton Tea was introduced to the American public.

18:40 | I guess you can say the Amerikanski's dug this tea. That's pretty much all I ever knew of growing up. They were the Kleenex of tea in my early days. They set up a company in New York that later moved to Hoboken, birthplace of Frank Sinatra. The Lipton Tea brand is owned since 1971, by the Anglo-Dutch giant, Unilever.

19:01 | Thomas Lipton personified the word "workaholic". He had a sign that hung on his wall that said, "There is no fun like work." You know, he never married and would joke when people would ask why he, the great multi-millionaire tea tycoon, had never gotten hitched. Lipton's pat reply was always, "Oh, the price of tea was far too low to keep a wife."

19:26 | By 1898 Lipton's company went public. The biggest IPO of its day. He only tried to raise two million pounds but the share offering was twenty-five times oversubscribed. Lipton was knighted by Queen Victoria that same year. Man, he was riding high!

THE TEA HISTORY PODCAST BOOK 2
PART 17

19:44 | Lipton by the way, was the original in a line of famous tycoons who financed yachts in the America's Cup, this oldest of all international sporting trophies. He bankrolled yachts in the 1899, 1901, 1903, 1914 and 1929 America's Cup. Lipton's team never won, but he was always particularly admired by the Yanks because of his excellent displays of good sportsmanship. These appearances in the America's Cup gave the Lipton brand a huge rocket boost during those decades. Alan Bond, Sir Michael Fay, Bill Koch and Larry Ellison all followed in Lipton's footsteps in using their financial might to win this coveted trophy.

20:35 | Lipton and James Taylor met in 1890 and with Lipton's money and management know-how and Taylor's success in growing tea in the highlands of Ceylon, this island began to join its neighbor India as a major world grower of quality black teas.

20:54 | The first seeds to be planted in Ceylon came from tea plants from Assam, the indigenous variety of *Camellia sinensis*. The British built the tea industry in Sri Lanka very much as they did in India. It's another great history and has spawned all kinds of stories and interesting people. The British did the same thing in Kenya, too. Kenya today is a major world producer of tea. It was brought there in 1903, back in the British colonial days. They brought tea to a lot of places.

21:27 | The stories are well-known about the virtual enslavement of millions who toiled on the mountainsides working on the tea plantations. This was the dirty seamy underside

THE TEA HISTORY PODCAST BOOK 2
PART 17

of the tea growing industry. This aspect was no less odious than the chapter on opium. It's a very well documented side of the history of tea.

21:50 By the mid to late 1800s, tea had become a mature and established global enterprise with major exchanges in several cities to buy and sell tea. Up until Fortune's time, tea had always been sort of a mom and pop industry despite the huge volumes of exports beginning in the 1800s. Of course, nowadays in China you have massive modern tea operations that manufacture bulk commodity grade teas using all the latest machinery.

22:21 But the quality remains in the artisanal tea trade. You'll see in all the web dealers of tea and in serious teashops, all the action is with quality loose leaf tea that is still being made in China the old-fashioned way.

22:37 As expected, China later got into the poppy growing and opium manufacturing business. That had an immediate effect on British opium exports. The EIC sent Fortune again as their agent to go check out the operation and procure samples of the China poppies for analysis.

22:58 After this consulting gig, Fortune was retained by the US government to assist them in building a tea operation in the southern United States. This involved another China trip where Fortune had to go bring back some more seeds. This whole trick had been thoroughly learned and perfected by this time.

THE TEA HISTORY PODCAST BOOK 2
PART 17

23:17 | Between March and August 1858 Fortune did his work for the Amerikanski's. But when he brought everything back his employers gave him his walking papers and said they'd take everything from there. According to what I read, Fortune ended up getting stiffed by the Yanks and they never paid him. And in the end all the hard work came to naught because when the US Civil War began a few years later in 1861, it wasn't the best time to be setting up a tea plantation in the south.

23:48 | Robert Fortune made one last trip to China in 1862. This one was as a private citizen. He also visited Japan, and in both places brought back the usual array of plant specimens and curiosities. He died in 1880 leaving an estate worth 40,000 pounds which in today's inflated world would come to about $5 million.

24:13 | Robert Fortune gets credit for more than acting as the tip of the spear in bringing Chinese tea plants and know how to India. He was the first to successfully bring hundreds of species of plants to England, among them: bleeding hearts, winter jasmine, white wisteria, twelve species of rhododendron and the chrysanthemum.

24:37 | Not too many people can say they proved the great Carl Linnaeus wrong, but Fortune did when he discovered green and black tea both came from a single species. And had it not been for Fortune observing all the poisonous additives being mixed in with the green tea supply from China, who knows who many lives might have been lost.

 THE TEA HISTORY PODCAST BOOK 2
PART 17

24:57 | Okay, that's all I got for you today. More next time I assure you. So please do consider coming back. I mean, you made it this far. You may as well stick around to the end.

25:07 | Don't forget over at the Website teacup.media you can find a list of all the Chinese terms used in this and every episode as well as a few different ways to support your humble narrator in all these podcasting endeavors. Once again that url is teacup.media.

25:27 | This here's Laszlo Montgomery signing off from Los Angeles, California. Do consider coming back next time for another episodio fascinante of the Tea History Podcast.

 **The Tea History Podcast
Book 2 Part 18**

THE TRANSCRIPTS

SUMMARY

In this episode, we focus on the category of tea that is most admired by many tea experts the world over. Pu-Erh tea was introduced sometime during the Ming Dynasty and in time, became the oft-called "King of Teas" for its rich and unique flavor, wholly unlike any other tea produced in China.

TRANSCRIPT

00:00 | Hi everyone, Laszlo Montgomery here of the Tea History Podcast, a close relative of the China History Podcast. Go check that show out if you're into that sort of thing. It's called one of the best podcast shows out there in the China history space.

00:14 | We're continuing on with our story, getting to the end.

00:17 | Thanks to the services of Mr. Robert Fortune and many others, by the late 1800s after tea plantations sprouted up all over northern India and Sri Lanka, tea planting then spread fast to Russia, Turkey, Kenya and other parts of Africa and Asia.

00:35 | After the secret became common knowledge, almost any country with the climate and geography entered the tea growing business. In 2021 there are at least forty-eight

THE TEA HISTORY PODCAST BOOK 2
PART 18

countries in the world producing tea now. As I said in the first episode, at three billion cuppa's a day, tea is the third most consumed substance on earth after air and water. But its penetration to almost every country on earth only happened in the 20th century.

01:04   You know, I haven't even spoken about Pǔ-Ěrh tea. I received no small amount of concerned emails from listeners asking me what kinds of Tea History Podcast is this. Eighteen episodes in and scant mention of Pǔ-Ěrh. And when the heck am going to get around to talking about this. The king of teas. The tea most appreciated by true experts, aficionados and chárén in all shapes and sizes.

01:37   Pǔ-Ěrh is not just a category of tea. It's also a place. It's now a prefecture-level city, a dìjíshì, located in southern Yúnnán province, about two hours north of Xīshuāngbǎnnà and five hours south of Kūnmíng.

01:47   Xīshuāngbǎnnà is a city south of Pu-erh. I guess people like to call that area of Yunnan the center of the epicenter as far as where Pǔ-Ěrh tea was first grown and made.

02:02   The Chama gudao, the Tea Horse Road, began in the south part of Xīshuāngbǎnnà in a place called Yìwǔ. Not to be confused with Yìwū in central Zhejiang province, center of the merchandise wholesale trade in China.

02:16   Pǔ-Ěrh's name, don't ask me why, was changed to Sīmáo in 1949, but ever since 2007 after Pǔ-Ěrh tea had become such a global sensation, they decided to change it back

THE TEA HISTORY PODCAST BOOK 2
PART 18

to the original name. The market in Pǔ-Ěrh tea promptly crashed soon afterwards, but we'll get to that.

02:37 What's interesting about Pǔ-Ěrh the city is that it borders three countries: Laos, Vietnam and Burma. The Shan State of Burma, so you know which famous Triangle Pǔ-Ěrh is located in. They get about fifty-nine inches of rain there a year, so you know that slice of Yúnnán is wet, humid, with lots of sunshine and carpeted with mountains and valleys. Perfect tea growing conditions. No wonder the epicenter of all the indigenous tea trees in the world is located in this province.

03:10 The tea that comes out of this region of southern Yunnan is so special that its own category had to be created just for it. In Cantonese they called this tea Bo Lay.

03:22 I mentioned in a previous episode about Yíxīng ware. Pǔ-Ěrh is the tea that goes hand in hand with that tea ware from Jiāngsū province. Why are some tea people so in love with Pǔ-Ěrh? I have to say, among Chinese teas, it has a taste all its own. It's very distinct and has been described as earthy, musty and very natural tasting.

03:50 I've met tea people who are simply reverent about Pǔ-Ěrh tea. All teas are unique in their own ways but Pǔ-Ěrh… how can I explain the way this tea stands out? The way it is processed and also in the terroir and special handling involved in the processing and storage makes Pǔ-Ěrh tea so special.

THE TEA HISTORY PODCAST BOOK 2
PART 18

04:12 You can make green tea almost everywhere in southern and central China. Same with almost any tea, I guess. But not Pǔ-Ěrh. No, not unless it's Yúnnán Dàyè big leaf tea, grown, processed, sun-dried in the time-worn fashion of the locals and packed in this region of southern Yúnnán can you call it Pǔ-Ěrh chá. There's no such thing as Fujian Pu-erh or Hangzhou Pu-erh.

04:41 Another unique thing about Pǔ-Ěrh tea is that, like red wine, this tea is considered better the older it gets. This isn't necessarily true in all cases of course, but an aged cake of Pu-erh is considered something special that you might enjoy ten, twenty or thirty years from now or maybe pass it down to the next generation or as it sometimes happens, sell it at auction.

05:08 And because some of this tea is so expensive, there's a big market in fakes. It's like this for all the top priced teas, not just Pǔ-Ěrh's. There's quite a brisk business in these counterfeit Shānzhài teas.

05:23 Another interesting thing about Pǔ-Ěrh tea is that although you can buy it in loose leaf form, its most characteristic type of packaging by far are these round, disc-like tea cakes and other shapes that were designed centuries ago specifically for ease in packing and transport.

05:43 The most well-known of these traditional ways to package Pǔ-Ěrh teas was in these discs, a few different sizes. They're shaped just like a discus. And seven of these discs would be stacked in a bamboo wrapper of

THE TEA HISTORY PODCAST BOOK 2
PART 18

sorts and these became known as qī zǐ bǐngchá or Seven Sons Tea Cake. You always see those characters on the wrapper of most of these Pu-erh disc-shaped tea cakes, and you can buy them individually. I have a couple dozen in my collection and I didn't purchase a single one. They were all gifts from my Chinese friends and colleagues. Pǔ-Ěrh tea cakes are very popular gifts.

06:21 Remember in an earlier episode we discussed the *Chámǎ gǔdào*, the Ancient Tea Horse Road? They'd load up on these tea bricks in Yunnan and Sichuan and to the west and to the north the tea would be transported. The minority ethnic people down there loaded up their wagons with the tea picked from these ancient trees, with their dàyèzǐ or big leaves, and supplied these regions beyond China's borders.

06:51 All the tea grown by these ethnic minority people in the nooks and crannies of the mountains around there would be taken to the central market of Pǔ-Ěrh City. There in Puerh City, the tea farmers and merchants would gather to start the ball rolling as far as getting the product out to the markets in Tibet, Mongolia and elsewhere.

07:12 The tea makers scattered among the many mountains of Yúnnán all make a similar product. But each brand of Pǔ-Ěrh has its own particular tèdiǎn or something about it that experts are most enamored by.

07:29 But this tea, it wasn't Pǔ-Ěrh tea yet. It was just dried and compressed tea leaves. Pǔ-Ěrh tea as we know it wouldn't make its debut until the Ming dynasty.

 THE TEA HISTORY PODCAST BOOK 2
PART 18

07:38 | Speaking in the most general terms possible, there are two types of Pǔ-Ěrh tea. Shēng Pǔ-Ěrh and Shóu Pǔ-Ěrh. Shēng means raw and shóu means ripe.

07:50 | There's two ways to make Ripe Pǔ-Ěrh tea. You can either do it the old-fashioned way and let it age or there was a processing method that only came in the 1970's that accelerates the ripening process. You see, this shows even into our modern times, tea still hadn't yet revealed all its secrets.

08:11 | The longer you age the pu-erh in storage, the better tasting and more mellow it becomes, and usually more expensive too. With ripe Pǔ-Ěrh, tea the green raw Pǔ-Ěrh's aging process is accelerated by this special process that spares you the thirty-year wait for that raw Pǔ-Ěrh to reach its optimum taste.

08:34 | This special process is called wòduī. Wò means to wet or to moisten. Duī means a heap or a pile. This is a process where the raw leaves are fooled into believing they are being aged slowly but in fact it all happens rather quickly and what you ultimately get is a pu-erh tea that is fully oxidized, microbiologically fermented and tasting quite old and venerable already.

09:04 | So you can obtain Pǔ-Ěrh tea as an already ripened, ready to drink *shóu* Pǔ-Ěrh or you can enjoy the raw or green Pǔ-Ěrh which has other characteristics to it which can be no less enjoyable, though most Pǔ-Ěrh people might not agree.

THE TEA HISTORY PODCAST BOOK 2
PART 18

09:21 | There's so many interesting things about Pǔ-Ěrh tea. Where it's made and who is making it is also quite fascinating. As I just mentioned, it's mostly all made down in Yunnan province. And last I checked, there are twenty-six different ethnic minority people down in Yúnnán and a lot of them are involved in the Pǔ-Ěrh tea business.

09:43 | The mass of Pǔ-Ěrh tea comes from bushes planted in great tea gardens. But some come from trees that are relatively young, that is, 100-200 years old. The more expensive and coveted pu-erh teas come from the older tea trees, many of them growing wild in the mountains of southern Yunnan. The trees only grow on the mountainsides. The older the tree, the more intense the taste.

10:10 | There's a type of Pǔ-Ěrh that's particularly prized and giving it as a gift to someone is quite special. These are the leaves that are picked from a gǔshù, or an ancient tree.

10:23 | In Chinese, Pǔ-Ěrh tea is also referred to as a Hēichá or a black tea. It has the darkest liquor of most all teas. For Ripe and Raw Pǔ-Ěrh, *shēng* pu-er and *shóu* Pǔ-Ěrh, they both start from the same leaf.

10:41 | Our Western nomenclature for Black tea, like Lipton for example, in the Chinese reckoning would actually be called hóngchá or red tea.

 THE TEA HISTORY PODCAST BOOK 2
PART 18

10:50 | So let's take a quick look at how they make Pǔ-Ěrh tea.

10:53 | After the tea pickers, these cǎichánü, have done their job, the front-end work is similar to any number of green teas.

11:02 | First, they are heaped into piles where a bacterial culture is added. And then it starts to do its thing. There's a lot of microbial activity involved in the production of Pǔ-Ěrh.

11:14 | The next thing done is to kill those dang enzymes that immediately start working on the plucked leaf the minute it hits the cǎichánü's tea basket. That's the *shā qīng* part. Remember *shā* means to kill and *qīng* means green. Big woks are used to pan-fry the leaves and immediately partially, but not totally, deactivate the enzymes.

11:37 | Next step is to roll those leaves, the róuniǎn part. This step is where the great masters who make all this artisanal hand-made tea do that thing they do, pounding, twisting and doing these other secret techniques that only they know about. This adds their little touch to their village's brand of pu-erh. The leaves are not rolled too aggressively or for long. The tea masters have their way of knowing how long to work those leaves. They know how to adjust everything, the temperature and humidity, and everything else that goes into the precise outcome of every individual tea flavor profile.

THE TEA HISTORY PODCAST BOOK 2
PART 18

12:22 No ovens or mechanical short-cuts are involved in making real Pǔ-Ěrh tea. Real Pǔ-Ěrh tea has to be sun-dried after rolling. Under that Yunnan sun it must go for further fermentation of the leaves to take place. Some places will allow them to dry in a special temperature and humidity-controlled room with just enough moisture to continue to allow for oxidation. And this can take as long as forty days.

12:52 Once this front-end processing is all taken care of, the end result is Raw Pu-er or *Máochá*. Máo, aside from being the same character *Mao* as in Chairman Mao, but here it means something else, semi-finished I presume, guessing from the multitude of different meanings for the character *Mao*.

13:14 *Máochá*, well, this is sort of like the stem cell. It could go either way depending on what you wish to do with it. This má*ochá* is very similar looking to green tea.

13:25 If you want to make shēng pu-erh, raw pu-erh, from this point you steam the *máochá*, mold it and wrap it up into any number of package forms. Once this is done, the product is called semi-fermented at this point.

13:40 The remainder of the fermentation will occur in the package over time, providing you keep the cake of Pǔ-Ěrh stored properly. I'm not going to get into the chemical details, but while you have it stored away in a cool, dark place, there's a whole microbiology lesson going on inside that Pǔ-Ěrh tea.

THE TEA HISTORY PODCAST BOOK 2
PART 18

14:02 | Any bacteriologists or mycologists out there wondering, the two chief culprits involved in the process are Aspergillus and Penicillium. Species pluralis, I might add. They're the predominant microbes working their magic.

14:18 | And if you just kick back and wait fifteen or twenty years, you'll have some nice mature Pǔ-Ěrh tea.

14:25 | But if you want the Ripe Pǔ-Ěrh, the stuff that tastes like it's been kept in a safe place for a nice stint, more has to be done to get it ready for the wòduī process that acts like a time machine bringing this Pǔ-Ěrh tea to a future state of maturity.

14:42 | Also, I may not have clearly explained the differences that exist between the Ripe Shú Pǔ'ěr tea aged naturally over decades and the ripe Pu'er tea that used the wòduī process developed in Yúnnán. This process, developed in the 1970's, lit a fire under the aging process and speeded things up. I just wanted to mention that amongst the cognoscenti who know their Pu'erh, there's a world of difference.

15:10 | This secret process was discovered at the Kūnmíng Chá Chǎng, the Kūnmíng Tea Factory, back when bell-bottoms were just beginning to go out of style. This process expedites the fermentation of the natural molds in the tea and turns the tea leaves black. A drying process follows where yeast and mold on the leaves continues to ferment. Mold actually appears on the leaf. You really have to get it right making ripe pu-erh tea. Otherwise,

THE TEA HISTORY PODCAST BOOK 2
PART 18

	you can end up with some pretty foul smelling and rancid tasting stuff.
15:45	After the fermented and post-fermented leaves are completely dried, workers will sift through the whole pile and take all the good full unbroken leaves and put those aside. That is the primo stuff.
16:01	From that point on, its two more steps. Sterilize everything and either sell it as-is, loose leaf product, or the final step is to compress it into any number of traditional shapes. The round bǐngchá discs are perhaps most common as well as the bird's nest-shaped *tuóchá*.
16:20	Most of the pu-erh tea I've seen is wrapped in a kind of paper that lists all the vital info of where it came from, weight, when it was packed and the brand. If the tea is one of those high value ones that have been sold, auctioned or passed on, the provenance is also shown on the wrapper. There's a system they have to authenticate all this.
16:44	Collectors in China, Hong Kong, Taiwan and Southeast Asia caused the prices of Pǔ-Ěrh tea to skyrocket in the lead-up to the Beijing Olympics when money was loose and there was a lot of it sloshing around the system. And corruption back then... was still sort of okay. Prices for the best Pǔ-Ěrh's were out of sight, but in 2008 the market crashed and the good folks down in Yunnan who were riding the crest of that Pǔ-Ěrh wave had to take a few gulps of xīběifēng, that northwest wind. Old saying: hē xīběifēng. So wretched and unpleasant are the winds coming off of the Gobi and across Xinjiang that

THE TEA HISTORY PODCAST BOOK 2
PART 18

to say you really got it rough one might say they are drinking the northwest winds.

17:29 Anyway, Pǔ-Ěrh tea, like white, green and oolong teas has become popular in the world of health products. Pu-erh and white teas, the two diametric opposites of the tea category spectrum, are these days touted as particularly healthy to drink.

17:48 Mind you, the health products industry is not regulated, so a lot of these claims that are made to the efficacy of these teas and tea extracts don't have anything like the FDA to keep them honest. We all have to just sort of take their word for it or do our own due diligence.

18:08 Pǔ-Ěrh tea has vitamins B1, B2, C and E, potassium, phosphorous, calcium, magnesium, aluminum, lysine, arginine, histidine, cystine, and trace amounts of zinc, sodium, nickel, iron, beryllium, sulfur and fluorides. Hey, who needs vitamins?

18:24 Practitioners of Traditional Chinese Medicine say Pǔ-Ěrh opens up the meridians and warms the middle burner inside you, namely your stomach and spleen. TCM researchers also maintain that Pǔ-Ěrh tea facilitates mental alertness and fights high cholesterol, obesity and diabetes, as well as containing the same antioxidants found in other teas that, through its blood cleansing properties, protects the heart and coronary system.

18:55 The claims made by some scientists or marketing people, not sure, regarding Pǔ-Ěrh tea's effectiveness as a

THE TEA HISTORY PODCAST BOOK 2
PART 18

weight-loss aid? Well, the jury is still out on that. And all of the reports that I've skimmed through on The Google, well, they were carried out on animals, not humans. Not that we're not mammals ourselves. Just sayin'.

19:15 But unlike other teas, it's said ripe, but not raw Pǔ-Ěrh tea, in particular contains lovastatin, something available only as a prescription drug used in slowing the production of cholesterol in your body. The riper the Pǔ-Ěrh the more lovastatin.

19:34 And more than any other tea, Pǔ-Ěrh is also considered the best digestive aid, especially after a nice heavy meal that may or may not be high in oils and fats. This may or may not come from the healthy probiotics you ingest that come about from the fermentation process. It's said Pǔ-Ěrh is the perfect tea to cap off a nice dim sum meal.

19:57 And though I myself, not being much of an imbiber of alcohol, can't claim this but many say that Pǔ-Ěrh tea is also a curative for hangovers.

20:07 Claims and research abound regarding Pǔ-Ěrh 's efficacy in breaking down fats and lowering LDL, bad cholesterol, as well as in the treatment of arteriosclerosis, colds, bleeding and hepatitis. And the high level of Vitamin C can be rapidly taken in by the body. Besides lowering fat and cholesterol, Pu-erh tea is also touted as effective in treating and preventing cancer. Hard to say at this point though.

THE TEA HISTORY PODCAST BOOK 2
PART 18

20:34 | There's way more to it than what I'm telling you. And the varieties of Pǔ-Ěrh tea go way beyond the ripe and raw leaves that I've mentioned. If you drill down a little deeper, you'll find it's very complex. And if you find it's not your cup of tea, keep trying.

20:54 | Search for any reputable looking online tea shop and you'll see dozens of different kinds of Pǔ-Ěrh teas: loose, in cake form, baby tips, raw, ripe, mixtures of raw and ripe and a myriad of brands and ages. There are so many YouTube videos showing how to prepare Pǔ-Ěrh and how to enjoy it to the max. There are videos of the most respected tea masters showing you how to do it up right, every step of the way.

21:23 | Pǔ-Ěrh tea might have a bit of an acquired taste. You never know, you may like it on the first try. If you've never tried it before, I hope this briefest of introductions gives you an idea about what it is and why real tea people who love Chinese tea wake up and go to sleep every night with this stuff. You'll see some online tea stores only deal with Pǔ-Ěrh and nothing else. I can only say if you never tried it before, give it a shot.

21:54 | And as I mentioned previously, if you should find Pǔ-Ěrh to your liking and want to make this your go-to tea for everyday use, make sure to invest in an Yìxīng teapot, which is really the best way to cuddle up to Pǔ-Ěrh tea. As I mentioned in that episode, these special teapots are perfect for this kind of tea. And the more you use them, the more the porous clay of the Yìxīng ware becomes seasoned by the brew and over time becomes one with

THE TEA HISTORY PODCAST BOOK 2
PART 18

the Pǔ-Ěrh tea flavor. And as I also mentioned, don't mix teas with your Yìxīng teapot. Keep it only for your Pǔ-Ěrh. That's what this kind of tea ware was developed for.

22:36 You'll see in all of these videos showing you the delights of Pǔ-Ěrh tea in every one, these masters and tea experts always use these Yìxīng teapots and deliver to you free of charge everything and anything you need to know: how to prepare the tea, how to take care of your Yìxīng teapot, how to store your Pǔ-Ěrh and just plain old, how to enjoy the whole experience.

23:04 And with Pǔ-Ěrh tea you can get five, six, seven and even more pours per serving. And some insist the Pǔ-Ěrh tea flavor reaches its optimal level after a certain number of pours. Everyone is different as far as what pleases them most and you can find out for yourself that perfect sweet spot when you're kicking back and enjoying Pǔ-Ěrh yourself or with your friends or loved ones.

23:29 I've only given the briefest of thumbnail overviews of what pu-erh tea is all about. Next episode we'll look at several more teas and some of the history and legends surrounding them. I'll try not to overwhelm you with all the different choices you have out there. It really is that. It's overwhelming. But it's a good overwhelming. So that's for next time.

23:51 Until then, fine fine friends all over this world, this is Laszlo Montgomery signing off from Los Angeles in the Golden State, wishing you all the best and giving you

THE TEA HISTORY PODCAST BOOK 2
PART 18

my highest recommendation to come back next time for an ambrosial episode of the Tea History Podcast.

The Tea History Podcast
Book 2 Part 19

SUMMARY

Today's Tea History Podcast episode will go from province to province and look at a variety of famous teas such as Longjing, Gunpowder, Huangshan Maofeng, Lu'an Guapian, Xinyang Maojian, Taiping Houkui and a few others. All of the teas to be introduced began their brilliant careers as tribute teas sent annually to the emperor. You too can savor these teas fit for an emperor by purchasing them online at any number of online (and offline) tea sellers.

TRANSCRIPT

00:00 Hi everyone, it's me again, Laszlo Montgomery bringing you another episode in our overview of the History of Tea, the topic from which we derived this catchy podcast title.

00:12 Welcome back all you stalwarts who have stuck with this since the trailer. I hope over the past eighteen episodes you've found something worthwhile in this humble effort to introduce the history of tea, with the disclaimer of course that this is the Chinese version. Tea history and stories of tea culture are present in all countries where tea is drunk. Sorry I couldn't get to any of them.... not yet anyway.

00:37 I'll try and tie up some loose ends and if I should come

THE TEA HISTORY PODCAST BOOK 2
PART 19

across any orphans of information that I neglected to put in previous episodes, we'll place them here or in the next episode.

00:49 I thought perhaps a good way to break this all down would be to travel from province to province in China and take a look at some of their more famous teas that you're apt to find in your typical teashop or online store. The most famous teas are more often than not former tribute teas from the Qing dynasty.

01:07 The ability to get your hands on tea and to enjoy it sure has come a long way since the treacherous times of the Tea-Horse Road and the days of the China Clippers of the 1850s and 60s. People had to go to a lot of trouble to get this stuff from China to their teapot.

01:26 In our time we go online and in five minutes place an order for any number of magnificent artisanal teas from reputable online firms from all over the world and have them delivered right to your door. Think of that as you peruse some of these websites. Man, we got it easy in our time. And like I said last time, an endless quantity of videos online to show you how to do it up right once that hermetically sealed bag of tea shows up at your door.

THE TEA HISTORY PODCAST BOOK 2
PART 19

01:56 | Let's talk a little about green tea first. That's where most of the action is in the China market. Western markets, in India and in other places, they may love their black teas. But in China about 70% of all the tea produced is green. Zhejiang, Jiangxi and Anhui are the three provinces most renowned for green tea.

02:19 | You'll notice when you line up a couple dozen or so different green teas from all over China, you'll see they all look different from each other. Different size, color, shape, leaf length. Some are just buds. Some a bud and a leaf or a bud and two leaves or leaves without buds. Some are twisted. Some are straight flat. Some are curved in crescent shapes. Over time, the more you study tea, the more you'll notice famous teas always have something about them that makes the leaves instantly identifiable.

02:54 | One thing that's confusing about these top-drawer teas is that even within a single kind of tea there are multiple grades. Remember how I explained in the Tribute Tea system that ran from Tang to Qing, the most prized of all teas were those picked before the Qingming Festival, before the rains of early April. You can buy this primo grade tea as well whenever it hits the market in April, May or June.

03:21 | If you're shopping online for, say, a Lóngjǐng tea, you'll see the number of choices are staggering. Even within the confines of one single online tea seller you might have half a dozen choices of Lóngjǐng available. You'll see so many choices available with a considerable difference in pricing. Is it pay more get more?

THE TEA HISTORY PODCAST BOOK 2
PART 19

03:45 | The Chinese, from time immemorial always knew about these first flushes picked before the spring rains, that yielded the best teas. The Europeans soon learned as well. Remember the great 19th century tea clipper races that happened? These vessels would race from Fuzhou to England as soon as the first teas were loaded on board and off they'd go. If you were the first to slide into that parking space at the port, your firm could fetch a gorgeous premium for every ounce of tea in your cargo hold. Today too, everyone who knows tea knows, this grade of tea is something special.

04:26 | There are other grades besides this first flush. So ordering artisanal whole leaf tea online is a very three dimensional task. The best thing to do is stick with the most reputable online tea shops until you're ready to wander off and try out other places. Like with pearls, jade and silk, it's easy to get ripped off when buying premium grade teas. The tea forums and blogs are most informative in the pointers that they offer where to get good stuff. I subscribe to the tea sub-Reddit and find that quite useful. Those Redditors are some of my top tea masters.

05:05 | Back to green tea. Lóngjǐng tea, I'll go out on a limb and say it's perhaps the most famous green tea in China. Dragon Well tea it's called. It comes from a place called Lóngjǐng Village not too far from West Lake in beautiful Hangzhou. I've been to Lóngjǐng Village. Bought some souvenir tea and everything.

THE TEA HISTORY PODCAST BOOK 2
PART 19

05:27 | There are about five districts in the area that produce authentic Lóngjǐng tea. What's so great about this tea?

05:35 | Well, these lucky tea farmers of Lóngjǐng back in the 18th century had gained sufficient repute in the region to the extent that one day they were visited by no less a personage than the Qianlong emperor himself.

05:48 | And that great tea-drinking emperor, grandson of another great tea-drinking emperor, himself planted eighteen tea bushes there in Lóngjǐng and later even picked some of the tea himself. So that's a heck of a story to have associated with your town. If an emperor so masterful in tea proclaimed your product superior and wrote a poem about how good it was to boot, your share price skyrocketed. Fame and fortune was guaranteed. I mean, come on, the Qianlong emperor? Chinese history? He's pretty big.

06:23 | About those eighteen trees, there's another story. This one, I don't know. But I'll tell it anyway. Remember back in those Qing dynasty overview episodes I mentioned how the Qianlong emperor was extremely devoted to his mother? It was when he was down in Hangzhou visiting Lóngjǐng village and picking tea that he learned that his mother was ailing back in the palace.

06:46 | So he cut short the tour and he hurried back north to be with her. And in the excitement of the moment, the emperor carelessly had stashed some Longjing tea leaves inside his royal sleeve. When he got back to the palace, well, you know what happened next. He discovered

THE TEA HISTORY PODCAST BOOK 2
PART 19

them, prepared the tea leaves for his sick mother and you guessed it. She made the comeback of the century and was on her feet in no time.

07:11 And so to honor this tea and those who grew it, he ordered these eighteen trees to be planted at Lóngjǐng village in a particular spot by Húgōng Temple and he stipulated that these trees should henceforth supply the palace with Lóngjǐng Dragon Well tea.

07:32 Today, if you want to buy any of this tea off of those eighteen trees, it'll run you about twenty-five grand US for a quarter ounce, or a hundred grams, if they even allow it anymore. Probably not.

07:45 The telltale sign or calling card of Lóngjǐng tea is its distinct shape. The leaves are beautiful, especially when you get a nice classic full bud set. They are pressed flat, as if pressed between the pages of a book. And when you infuse the tea you're really going to want to have a clear glass tea service because the Dragon Well tea leaves open up real nicely and are comforting and pleasurable to groove on when you're enjoying your Lóngjǐng moment.

08:18 The legend goes the leaves are all flat because on the ride back to Beijing, the Qianlong emperor had inadvertently pressed the leaves he had stashed in his sleeves for most of the ride back. So they ended up in that condition. Hey, who knows?

THE TEA HISTORY PODCAST BOOK 2
PART 19

08:33 You have to be a little vigilant when you brew Longjing tea. My suggestion, if you want the perfect cuppa, is to go watch a video on YouTube or Youku and there are scores to choose from, showing the best way to make Longjing tea. By all means, you don't want to scald these tea leaves. Green teas do not require fully boiled hot water. Longjing tea, like any of the greats, is really something else when brewed at optimum conditions.

09:03 One more thing, because of its popularity and all the legends and stories associated with it, Longing is often imitated and faux-Longjing is readily available in the market. It looks like Longjing. But it isn't. And most people, like me, don't know any better just by looking. Faux-Longjing can be had in Yunnan, Guizhou and a lot of it comes from Sichuan. Also Guangdong grows this, too. It's just processed like Lóngjǐng and sold with a Lóngjǐng label. As I said, most of the unsuspecting won't know any difference.

09:42 Another thing I heard when I was in Sichuan was that a lot of Sichuan tea gets shipped to Zhejiang where it is then processed into a faux-Lóngjǐng. Just know that many of these top grade Famous Teas in China, not just Longjing, command a high market price so naturally you get all these Shānzhài teas, these counterfeit lookalikes.

10:07 You'll hear the words *máojiān* and *máofēng* a lot when searching through many online stores and through tea guides. A lot of the teas out there are something or other *máojiān* or *máofēng* and these terms refer to any tea that consists of a bud and a single leaf only. In the case of

 THE TEA HISTORY PODCAST BOOK 2
PART 19

máojiān, jiān means the tip, the tip of the tea leaf, the youngest part. And *máofēng* means the bud plus the top two leaves. And for each individual kind of tea, the buds, the leaves should all pretty much look the same and be uniform in their appearance. And as I just mentioned if it's a *máojiān* tea, there's only one leaf and one bud.

10:54 Let's look at Gunpowder tea next. Also from Zhejiang Province. Another green tea that is somewhat well-known in the Western world because of its catchy name. It's processed in such a way that the leaves are rolled into these little balls or pellets, hence the name. For this reason, the Chinese call this tea and other ball or pellet shaped teas: *zhūchá*. Zhū means pearl.

11:21 Because it is rolled by hand, the leaves have to be a little bigger than what you might pick in the spring. The leaves picked in the summer and autumn, being larger in size, work best for this kind of tea.

11:34 Nowadays only the highest-end Gunpowder teas are rolled by hand. There are machines that can mimic this hand process pretty well and this is how most commodity Gunpowder tea is made.

11:46 The smaller the pellet, the higher the grade. The smaller the pellet, the harder it was to roll it, too. The smallest sized pellets of Gunpowder tea are known as Imperial Pinhead Gunpowder Tea. You'll see this on a lot of online tea shops.

THE TEA HISTORY PODCAST BOOK 2
PART 19

12:04 | There are multiple grades of this tea as well, all with quite a disparity between prices and grades. Traditionally this tea comes from Píngshǔi south of Shàoxīng, as I said, prosperous Zhèjiāng province, a place of so many renowned green teas.

12:23 | One thing famous about this Gunpowder tea is that this is the base tea used for the famous and totally refreshing Moroccan Mint tea. This is a nice easy tea to start with if you're just beginning to explore green tea. And another thing, just like with Lóngjǐng, Dragon Well tea, get yourself a nice clear glass teacup and watch those pellets unfurl as they steep away in all their glory.

12:52 | Gunpowder tea, like Bohea, Hyson, Congou is another one of the great historic teas of the 19th century.

13:01 | For all these teas I've mentioned and will mention, again I wanted to throw a few names at you. There are so many videos and blogs that can teach you so much. There are countless books and videos that lay it out for you from beginning to end. How hot the water should be, how much tea to add, how long to steep, utensils, tea ware, the whole ball of wax.

13:25 | Another famous green tea. Huángshān Máofēng. Ah, máofēng, so we know right away, hearing those two syllables, this one has the bud and the two top leaves next to the bud. This is the classic tea bud set. The historic granite peaks of Huángshān? Well, that says right away that this tea comes from Anhui province.

THE TEA HISTORY PODCAST BOOK 2
PART 19

13:46 | Like with many of China's most sacred mountains, if the climate is right for tea, tea is grown there. Of all the provinces in China, no one has more varieties of tea than Anhui. This tea, Huángshān Máofēng or Yellow Mountain Hair Tip, is the most famous tea of Anhui province. Like with Lóngjǐng tea, there are multiple grades sold at different prices and copious amounts of counterfeits.

14:12 | I have a long-time listener, surnamed Cáo, who's located in Anhui province. And he's from the city of Lù'ān. And he is the one who informed me of their famous Lù'ān Guāpiàn green tea. Lù'ān Guāpiàn also goes by the name Melon Seed tea. Guāpiàn means melon seed. This is one of those teas that has a distinct look about it and when the leaves open up they have the uniform appearance of melon seeds, like from a watermelon.

14:43 | I had some with my good friend Clement last time when we did our little tea excursion at some Cháchéng in Shanghai, a Tea City. Those are retail malls populated exclusively by people in the tea business. Leaves, teaware. It's like walking around Tea Heaven....

15:00 | Now, that's a great place to spend an afternoon. I don't know if I've ever run across one here in the US. With so many immigrants from China these past ten years or more, the number of shops has gone from not so many to all over the place. But regardless whether it's at a tea shop in a strip mall to one of these multi-level structures, maybe 2-3-4 stories high, it's a great place to hang, try out different teas and sample before you buy. And the

THE TEA HISTORY PODCAST BOOK 2
PART 19

person behind the counter making it for you, they know how to brew the perfect cup.

15:35 In San Francisco Chinatown, there are teashops that offer a couple hundred kinds of teas and you can sit there and sample some of them out. I spent a nice enjoyable hour at Vital Tea Leaf on Grant Street. These kinds of places are great for sampling teas. You can buy whatever you like with experts to guide you through the process.

15:56 If you're shopping for loose tea, you'll find most of these shops in these various Chacheng *plazas*, all have specialization. For example, one store will specialize in Yán chá, these rock teas from northern Fujian's Wǔyí Mountains. Some only deal in Pu-erh. I went to a place, it was a guy from Henan and he mostly carried the specialty of his province Xìnyáng Máojiān. This green tea is grown near the southern tip of Henan about a three-hour ride north of Lù'ān across the Anhui-Henan border.

16:33 I sat at this guy's shop and he made us both a pot of Lù'ān Guāpiàn and also his personal pride, Xìnyáng Máojiān. This Máojiān tea tells you it's quite delicate. Just one bud and one leaf. Xìnyáng Máojiān also goes by the name Xìnyáng Fur Tip. Mao meaning hair or fur, Jian, again, meaning tip.

17:00 If you're wondering how they grow tea all the way up there in Henan province, so was I. If you look at a map of China, Henan province is sort of north central, far north of the Yangzi. Well, this Xìnyáng Máojiān Tea,

 THE TEA HISTORY PODCAST BOOK 2
PART 19

one of the ten most famous in China, is also one of the most northerly spots in China where tea is grown. These climes this far north are not meant to grow tea. Xìnyáng is fifteen hundred miles north of Xīshuāngbǎnnà in Yunnan, where optimal tea growing conditions are said to be. So this, among other things is one of Xìnyáng Máojiān Tea's claim to fame.

17:44 About an eight to ten hour car ride due west of Xìnyáng in the farthest southeast corner of Shǎnxī province lies the city of Ānkāng, China's Land of Folk Songs. Not a very well-known place, I know. Their history goes all the way back to the Western Jìn.

18:00 And in this place too, so far north of the most ancient tea gardens of Shen Nong's time, believe it or not, tea is also grown. In nine counties of Shǎnxī province they produce tea. And the superstar of this province is their Zǐyáng Máojiān from Zǐyáng county near Ānkāng.

18:22 The good people there who make this tea boast that it is particularly high in selenium. This is something we all need in trace amounts to manufacture antioxidant compounds in our bodies to help with cellular function. Selenium, or Xī as it's called in Mandarin, also aids our immune system.

18:41 I haven't been offering you my worthless comments on how each tea tastes. I'm letting you know about the existence of these teas, their place in Chinese history and best of all to let you know that they are affordable and easily obtainable from little sample sizes up to 15 grams

THE TEA HISTORY PODCAST BOOK 2
PART 19

	to as much as you want or as much as what's available in the market.
19:04	Another well-known Anhui green tea is called Tàipíng Hóukuí. Another entry in China's Top Ten. This tea comes from about five hours north of Huángshān, Yellow Mountain.
19:17	Each great and famous tea usually has a story associated with it. This one says that the Hóukuí or Monkey King perished at this spot near Tàipíng Lake in Anhui and a farmer came upon the fallen Monkey King and buried him. Then the Monkey King's spirit in appreciation of the farmer's kindness, allowed for these tea trees to spring forth from where he had been interred.
19:46	This farmer reverently harvested and processed the leaves in a special and unique way and the acclaim for his tea reached all the way to the Imperial Palace in Beijing. And though this farmer never lived to see it, his tea won the grand prize at the World Expo in Panama in 1915 when they opened the canal.
20:06	This is a very rural part of Anhui where Tàipíng Hóukuí tea comes from. There are only about three villages that make this stuff. Real true-blue Tàipíng Hóukuí with its larger than average leaves is not easy to get. When it's available online it sells out fast.
20:27	This particular tea gets its appearance in the way it's specially processed. These leaves come out looking nice and flat and slightly embossed from the special leaves

THE TEA HISTORY PODCAST BOOK 2
PART 19

of paper or screens they are pressed between to air out. This is an all-hand operation.

20:46 And again, keep that clear teacup handy because these long leaves, when they unfurl and stand up straight at the bottom of your cup are really a sight to enjoy and meditate to. Vladimir Putin is said to be a fan of Tàipíng Hóukuí. Nuff said.

21:06 So as you can see when you sort everything out like I tried to do, the pricing out in the market is all over the place. But one thing rings true, the good stuff is costly. And if you're not going to go out of your way to use good water and brew it in a nice kettle and go all out, you may as well not buy the best grades.

21:26 You can try any of these and most of the online tea retailers will carry these greens. If you live near a teashop, for sure they will carry these.

21:38 Let's touch on white tea again. I mentioned in Part 4 about white tea and how hot the beverage market is these days. As I said, Fujian province is the home of authentic white tea as well as in parts of Yunnan.

21:52 Among the most famous White Teas are Fujian Silver Needle and Yunnan Silver Needle. They make it in India, Kenya now and elsewhere. I believe I've only ever imbibed on the Fujian variety.

22:06 I'd say the two most famous and readily available white teas are Bái Mǔdān or White Peony and Báiháo Yínzhēn

THE TEA HISTORY PODCAST BOOK 2
PART 19

Silver Needle tea. It's also marketed as White Pekoe Silver Needle Tea.

22:22 Silver Needle tea is considered the first white tea. It came out in the late Qing Dynasty. It's one of my favorite teas and a very distinct look. It's only made from the tea buds. No leaf. Just pure flavor and complexity. You'll get a nice caffeine buzz from this Silver Needle Tea.

22:43 Like any bud tea, you have to pick a lot of buds to equal a kilo of tea. It's not cheap but certainly affordable. In a quick spot check of Báiháo Yínzhēn Silver Needle Tea on Amazon, I saw it going for about $14 an ounce. I love this tea.

23:02 White Peony, Bái Mǔdān, is probably more widespread. Pound for pound grade for grade, it's about half the price of Silver Needle. It contains buds and leaves and isn't as light and subtle as Silver Needle. It's harvested after the Silver Needle buds have been picked.

23:22 The stuff available online in a thousand different places varies from top of the line from reputable names to low- and medium grade. It's all up to you. You can have a thoroughly pleasant and enjoyable Bái Mǔdān moment with so-so stuff. Depends how expert or selective you are in your tastes.

23:42 It was created after the fall of the Qing as an export tea. The pricing on white teas is similar to green. Not going to break the bank. If you're drinking tea for the catechins, also called "cat-a-kins" white teas, being the

THE TEA HISTORY PODCAST BOOK 2
PART 19

least processed with little or no oxidation offers you the highest catechin, antioxidant count. In general, the darker the tea, the lower the antioxidant count.

24:11 One more, and I'm very attached to this one. Me and my mate going back to 1980, Mr. W.W. Wong, we used to have Yam Cha all the time at Fuk Lam Mun on Kimberley Road in Tsim Sha Tsui. I had an office right around the corner from there, in his building in fact. He turned me on to Shòu Méi or Longevity Eyebrow tea. This is another white tea that consists of older tea leaves, harvested in the summer. For all the years I drank it with W, I didn't even know this tea was classified as a white tea. I thought it was an Oolong. Alas not. It's classified as a white tea, and you can also buy it in brick form like Pǔ-Ěrh.

24:54 And rather than start yapping away about Oolong Tea, let's close down the shop for now and save that for next time. So until then, me little beauties, this is Laszlo Montgomery signing off from LA. See if you can make it back next time for what's surely going to be another pretty exciting episode of the Tea History Podcast.

The Tea History Podcast
Book 2 Part 20

SUMMARY

We continue on with a tour of the provinces, looking at some of the more renowned teas each place has to offer. Teas such as Dancong, Tieguanyin, Jinjunmei, and Da Hong Pao are introduced. Various teas from Guangdong, Guangxi, Guizhou, Jiangsu, Jiangxi, Sichuan, Hubei, and Hunan are discussed.

TRANSCRIPT

00:00 | Hey everyone, for the twentieth time. Here I am, at your service. Laszlo Montgomery here with another good one from the Tea History Podcast.

00:08 | Last time we convened, I was just about to start introducing some of the more famous Oolongs that came out of China.

00:16 | Oolong Teas. There's so many to choose from. China Oolong tea primarily comes from Taiwan and Fujian. In Fujian, there are the famous Rock Teas or Yánchá of the Wǔyí Mountains where so much tea history happened. These are quite popular with the experts and amateurs like me too. These are among my favorites.

00:40 | Then in the south of Fujian you have Tiěguānyīn Tea of Ānxī. Then further south of there you get into

00:51 Guangdong province where they make Dāncōng tea.

Dāncōng. It's not a Yánchá, a Rock tea, but it's a nice Oolong and I'll get on that proverbial limb and say it's far and away the most famous Oolong grown in Guangdong province. Dāncōng comes from a place called Phoenix Mountain, Fènghuáng Shān, just north of historic Cháozhōu and Shàntóu. So you can be sure it's a heavy favorite of everyone from that region. And I'm guessing amongst the Hakka's in and around Méixiàn too.

01:23 I believe in all of Guangdong province, this must be that province's most famous tea. A very beloved Oolong. And you'll see with Dancing Tea, there are so many different flavor profiles and so many different grades of this tea.

01:38 Something else that's special about Dāncōng teas are that they come from trees, not bushes. And you need to wait until the trees are almost sixty years old before they're ready for action. And true blue, authentic Dāncōng theoretically comes from a single tree or more commonly a single mother tree that provided all the cuttings needed to replant in the same tea garden or grove, offering consistency to the flavor.

02:05 I have someone who used to work for me from Shàntóu. And she brought me the occasional baggy of top grade Dāncōng from her own personal stash that she gets from her relatives back home.

THE TEA HISTORY PODCAST BOOK 2
PART 20

02:18 | Tiěguānyīn comes from both Fujian and Taiwan. Its English name is usually Iron Buddha Tea. Guānyīn, of course, the beloved Goddess of Mercy. A lot of people pray to her. One version of the story concerning how this tea got its name, Tiěguānyīn is because the tea is black like iron, *tiě*, and pure and beautiful like Guānyīn.

02:43 | Another story goes that in Shāxiàn outside the city of Sānmíng in Fujian province, there was this old Buddhist temple with an iron statue of Guānyīn inside. The temple was all run down and everyone in Shāxiàn was so poor no one could afford to rebuild it. But one of the locals went in twice a month to help clean it up and worship. And they would burn incense to the goddess. One night the goddess Guānyīn appeared to him in a dream and told him to look inside this certain cave near the temple to seek a treasure that she had placed there for him to thank him for his devotion.

03:23 | He woke up the next morning and went to go search the cave. In it, he found a single tea shoot which he planted and took care of for several years. And when this bush was mature enough to yield its riches, the man discovered a fantastic brew. Cuttings were taken from this bush and were planted all around the area including in Ānxī, just a few hours away by car. Within a generation everyone in this region of Fujian prospered from growing this Tiěguānyīn Chá, as it became known. Iron Buddha or Goddess of Mercy Tea.

04:00 | One thing about Oolongs, you really get a lot of bang for your buck. This varies a great deal depending on

THE TEA HISTORY PODCAST BOOK 2
PART 20

multiple factors, but generally speaking you'll get 2-3 brews out of a serving of most green and white teas. And that third steeping is going to be very light. But with Oolongs, you can get as many as six to seven brews before they start to lose their distinctive flavor.

04:26 Jīnjùnméi, Golden Beautiful Eyebrow. This is another very popular tea these days. It's a Rock tea from Tongmu Village, Wǔyí Mountains. Only the yátóu, the buds, are used for this tea. So it's very delicate looking to behold.

04:43 Unlike other Oolongs, the tea buds are fully oxidized, which technically makes Jīnjùnméi a black tea rather than an Oolong. This bud-only tea will set you back $12 to $700 an ounce if that gives you any idea how much depth of quality there is in this and many other artisanal teas of this region. I randomly checked a good tea website and they had real Jīnjùnméi tea for $35 for four ounces. $8.75 an ounce.

05:16 The other more famous of the Yánchá Rock teas of Wǔyí Mountain are Ròuguì, Dà Hóng Páo, Tǐeluóhàn and one of my personal faves, Shǔixiān. There's also Shǔi Jīn Guī, and Bái Jī Guān. These are some of the main ones.

05:34 A lot of tea lovers swear by these Rock Teas of the scenic Wǔyī Mountain area. Again, having tried a few myself, I concur with this thinking. Like all these teas I've mentioned, they're all affordable and not going to set you back too much. And if you want to figure the cost on a per cup basis, compared to coffee, it's a bargain, especially if you get more than one single steeping.

THE TEA HISTORY PODCAST BOOK 2
PART 20

06:00 I mentioned Dà Hóng Páo. Great Red Robe or Big Red Robe Tea. Now this one has a story or two attached to it. Dà Hóng Páo is a tea admired by tea people the world over. A very very renowned tea. I love this stuff and like to keep a supply for every once in a while.

06:23 The history of Dà Hóng Páo goes all the way back to the Song but it achieved particular fame during the Ming dynasty. There's so many legends with this tea, I don't know where to begin.

06:35 The most famous story says that there was this poor scholar on his way to the Imperial Palace to sit for the civil service exams. He got sick along the way in the Wǔyí Mountain area and chanced upon a monk who took him in and nourished him at the monastery with this tea, their local brew. The scholar was able to recover and then made his way to the Palace where, legend has it, he scored the highest of all the candidates that year.

07:03 And also at the same time the scholar was present in the capital, the mother of one of the Ming emperors was ailing and not expected to make it. Luckily this scholar still had some of this tea that the monks had given him. The emperor's mother was given some of this brew and wouldn't you know it, it was just like with the Qianlong Emperor's mum and the Dragon Well Tea. She recovered from her illness. And so, the emperor, to express his sincerest gratitude sent a red robe to the monastery in appreciation, to cover these three tea bushes that the Dà Hóng Páo came from.

THE TEA HISTORY PODCAST BOOK 2
PART 20

07:41 Another version says the scholar, in appreciation for the way the monks took care of him and for facilitating all his success in the imperial exams, presented his red scholar's robes to them to be placed on the three tea bushes. There's many other stories, all quite hard to believe but they all go something like this and end with a big red robe being offered to honor and respect this great Yánchá, this rock or cliff tea.

08:09 I didn't get into too much detail about Taiwan's great teas. I mentioned in an earlier episode about John Dodd and Lǐ Chūnshēng playing key roles in the 1860's in developing Taiwan's tea export industry. Taiwan is famous for Oolongs although black and green teas are also grown there. But it's Taiwan's Oolongs that win all the prizes and are considered among the best.

08:36 Let's look at a few more provinces and their famous teas. Guìzhōu I didn't talk too much about. Quiet little Guìzhōu is today the second largest tea producing province in China and as far as green tea production, they're number one. Guìzhōu is famous for their Dūyún Máojiān which comes from Dūyún, about two hours by car west of the capital Guìyáng. Máojiān, again we all know now, simply means there's only a bud and a single leaf. And this green tea is not going to set you back a lot of money.

09:10 Among the stories Dūyún Máojiān has to tell, besides being Guìzhōu's most famous tea, is that supposedly it was named by The Great Helmsman himself, Chairman Mao. As the story goes, prior to being called Dūyún

THE TEA HISTORY PODCAST BOOK 2
PART 20

Máojiān, it was known as Yúgōu Chá, Fish Hook Tea because of the hooked shape of the dried buds. Well, some of this local tea was presented to Mao as a gift and so delighted was he, Mao re-named Yúgōu Chá as Dūyún Máojiān Chá.

09:45 The locals will tell you among its characteristics are the "three yellows". The leaves, the tea liquor, and a taste that they describe as yellow. Like other máojiān teas, it has the name fur tip in its English name. So it's also marketed as Dūyún Fur Tip tea.

10:05 Guizhou's other famous teas are Guìdìng Yúnwù chá and Méitán Cuìyá. All greens. Yúnwù means clouds and fog or clouds and mist. So you'll also see it marketed as Guìdìng Clouds and Mist Tea. The Méitán Cuìyá tea is sold as Guizhou Emerald Tips. If some of you recall from many years ago I bought some of this particular tea and sold it through one of my tea trade partners via the China History Podcast.

10:37 Now let's take a look at one of Guizhou's next-door neighbors. Guǎngxī is most famous for their Liùbǎo black tea. Actually Liùbǎo it's closer to Pǔ-ěrh than red tea because they do a kind of *wòduī* post-fermentation process. Liùbǎo is in the eastern part of Guangxi near the border with Guangdong. It's a small township, very remote and it's not that easy to get to.

11:03 They make this special tea up there in Liùbǎo but demand far exceeds what they can produce so Liùbǎo tea is sort of a type that is produced in many of the

THE TEA HISTORY PODCAST BOOK 2
PART 20

surrounding areas of Liùbǎo. Chinese immigrants who worked the tin mines in Malaysia in the 1890s and into the 20th century will remember this tea that was shipped in big quantities to the workers there. Liùbǎo, like every tea I mentioned, has multiple grades so you get what you pay for.

11:34 Remember last episode when I discussed Pu-erh tea I mentioned they discovered this *wòduī* process in the 1970s and it revolutionized the Pu-erh tea industry? It's said that the good people in Yunnan learned this *wòduī* process from the tea masters up in in Liùbǎo.

11:53 I've been told on good authority, if you want to get the full Liùbǎo tea cultural experience, don't go to Guangxi. Word on the street is that Malaysia is the place where this type of tea is particularly popular and still widespread and ingrained in the tea culture there.

12:14 Maybe six hours away by car from Liùbǎo to the west, about halfway to the Guangxi capital of Nanning, is the city of Guìpíng. For those of you who listen to the China History Podcast, you're probably familiar with this historic city. This is where the Taiping Heavenly Kingdom had its beginnings. It was there in Guìpíng where Hóng Xiùquán and his fellow rebels began to organize. They make Guìpíng Xīshān tea there. This is a green tea of Guangxi. Liùbǎo and Guìpíng Xīshān are probably the two best known Guangxi teas.

THE TEA HISTORY PODCAST BOOK 2
PART 20

12:52 Guìpíng Xīshān tea, like so many we've mentioned going back to Wú Lǐzhēn's time, all had their humble beginnings in Buddhist temples. Xǐshí Ān is a temple there in Guìpíng built during the early Qīng. And Guìpíng Xīshān tea is their famous offering to the world of great China green teas.

13:16 Let's move on to Sichuan. Wú Lǐzhēn, during the midway point of the first century BCE planted the seven tea plants on Méngdǐng shān. He's credited with getting everything started in Sichuan province as far as the tea industry was concerned. Remember the story of the famous Gānlù tea? It was called Gānlù Tea because it was cultivated during the Gānlù Era. It was one of the seven eras of the Han Emperor Xuān. Sichuan is famous for green teas, black teas and for all those tea bricks or biānchá that we spoke about in the earlier episodes of this tea series. It's also famous for tea culture.

13:57 When I was last in Sichuan, I stayed in Chengdu for about a week and checked out the tea scene up close. Someone took me to Rénmín Gongyuan. People's Park. I opted out of having my ears cleaned but while I was there I did have myself a nice Chángzuǐhú experience.

14:16 I didn't mention the Chángzuǐhú. This is one of my favorite little slivers of Chinese tea culture. It originated somewhere in the eastern part of Sichuan towards the end of the Qing, beginning of the Republican era. I don't know if you've ever seen one of them before. The pots that I have seen were all made of copper.

153

THE TEA HISTORY PODCAST BOOK 2
PART 20

14:37 Cháng means long and zǔi means mouth or in this case a spout of a teapot. And a hú mean a teapot. So Chángzuǐhú, a long spout teapot.

14:50 So the defining characteristic of this teapot is its long spout, about thirty-three inches or eighty-five centimeters. I read one of the purposes of the long spout was to offer the tea a chance to cool as it made its way out the other end and into the customer's tea cup.

15:09 The thing about this whole art is that there are about eighteen popular kung fu poses that the one dispensing the tea will use when they pour it into your cup.

15:22 With each pour, they dramatically and stylistically pose in these many kung fu stances and they pour the tea into your cup from behind their back, over their head, twisting sideways and in all kinds of other poses.

15:37 And each time they would refill your cup out that thirty-three inch spout right into your little teacup on the table and nary a drop is spilled. I'm a sucker for a Chángzuǐhú performance. The first time I saw that was in 1990 in Beijing at a Sichuan restaurant. I think it was at Dòuhuāzhuāng 老四川豆花莊. It just blew me away. And here I am, more than three decades later, still talking about it.

16:16 Sichuan is sort of a general term for the province. Chongqing does it this way and in Chengdu they do it that way. Some parts of Sichuan are mostly all ethnic minority people. It's a huge province. Used to be over 120

THE TEA HISTORY PODCAST BOOK 2
PART 20

million people living there until Chongqing was peeled away and made a municipality in 1997, reporting direct to Beijing. There are still more than 80 million people living in Sichuan province. That's about a quarter of the entire US population.

16:39 Frankly, not until I began to seriously study tea, did I ever look upon Sichuan as much of a tea place. So bright does the tea light shine in China's eastern provinces of Zhejiang, Jiangsu, Fujian and Anhui, where Chinese tea is concerned, Sichuan these days may seem like an afterthought.

17:01 In parts one, two and three you were able to see how critical Sichuan was in taking the initial baby steps to establish the art of tea in China. It all began in Sichuan. In the first episode, I called Sichuan the yuántóu for tea in China and therefore the world. It was also the center of the Chámǎ Gǔdào, the Ancient Tea Horse Road.

17:27 The contribution of Sichuan's tea farmers and tea artisans, especially in the early days was so critical to the evolution of tea. Those tea masters in Sichuan would patiently, season after season, gradually turn that bitter tú into sweet chá. Fortunately the Yangzi River ran right through this breadbasket of China. And eastward along the Yangzi River Valley this expert knowledge flowed.

18:00 The most famous teas of Sichuan all came out of the Méngdǐng Mountain area. Méngdǐng shān Xuěyá is a rare Yellow Tea. In English this would be Mt. Méngdǐng Snow Buds. Xuěyá means snow bud.

THE TEA HISTORY PODCAST BOOK 2
PART 20

18:18 | The other better known Sichuan teas are Méngdǐng Gān Lù or Méngdǐng Sweet Dew tea. There's also Zhúyèqīng or Bamboo Green tea, Qīngchéng Shān Snow Bud, É'méi Shān Máofēng, and É'Méi Shān Bái Yá. Báiyá means white bud. É'Méi shān, Mt. É'Méi, of course, one of the four sacred mountains of Buddhism. Tea is grown there. All of these teas from Sichuan can easily be purchased online.

18:48 | In Lù Yǔ's Classic of Tea, he mentions about fifty teas and of those fifty about 40% of them came from Sichuan.

18:56 | Another one of the most popular of the great and famous teas of China is Bìluóchūn from Jiangsu province near the Lake Tài area. I'd say that'd have to be that province's entry for best-known tea. Bìluóchūn translates to Green Snail Spring. It's one of those gorgeous little bud set teas that appear all tiny, twisted and curly like the meat you pull out of a snail's shell with a toothpick, for anyone who's ever enjoyed that. It's a green tea. This one's maybe a little more expensive than your average artisanal green teas, but not by much. And again, on a per cup basis, it's still cheaper than coffee by a mile. It's said that the Kāngxī emperor himself named this tea.

19:44 | Now, don't go carve this on your wall or anything, but Lóngjǐng, Lù'ān Guāpiàn and Bìluóchūn are considered the three top of the pops as far as China's most famous and admired green teas go. I would say go find your own top three. But these three, they sure get the most shine.

THE TEA HISTORY PODCAST BOOK 2
PART 20

20:05 Jiāngxī province doesn't get the respect it deserves. Their Best in Show is probably Míng Méi. This tea is grown in Wùyuán County just east of Jǐngdézhèn and south of Huáng Shān, Yellow Mountain. This is northernmost Jiangxi province. This is another of those *méi* teas. *Méi* means eyebrow. Teas that have that slender delicate arch to the dried leaves are often called something or other *méi*. I just mentioned Jīnjùnméi, Golden Beautiful Eyebrow tea...

20:41 Tea from this part of Jiangxi, in Wùyuán County, has been enjoyed by all the royals in the imperial palace since the time of the Song Dynasty. So this one goes way back, even to the Tang, because Lù Yǔ praised this tea.

20:57 Hey remember, Tàipíng Hóukuí that won that award at the 1915 World Expo in Panama? Well, Wùyuán Míngméi tea won a gold medal there also. I don't know, perhaps it was one of those things where everyone got an award. Wùyuán was once crowned the most beautiful village in China, I'll have you know.

21:17 The other big tea from Jiangxi is Lúshān Yúnwù. Lúshān Cloud and Mist. Lúshān of course one of the most historic cities in PRC and Communist Party history. This tea comes from Jiǔjiāng on the western side of Lake Póyáng. Lúshān Yúnwù has been a tribute tea since the time of the Song.

21:37 Zhū Dé himself, after tasting this famous tea of Jiangxi province was inspired to write a poem, "Lúshān yúnwù chá, wèi nóng xìng pōlà, ruò dé chángshí yǐn, yánnián

THE TEA HISTORY PODCAST BOOK 2
PART 20

yìshòu fǎ." The flavor of Lúshān yúnwù tea is strong and intense. If you drink it for long it is a way to attain longevity. (庐山云雾茶，味浓性泼辣，若得长时饮，延年益寿法). Zhū Dé, ladies and gentleman, founder of the Red Army. Lived to the age of 89 so he knew what he was talking about when endorsing this famous tea of Jiāngxī province.

22:14 I still haven't mentioned Húběi and Húnán. Plenty of tea is grown there too. In between Yíchāng and Jīngmén in Húběi is the county of Yuán'ān. This is where Hubei's famous yellow tea Yuǎn'ān Lù Yuàn is grown. Yuán'ān is the name of the county and Lùyuán is the name of a temple there.

22:36 The other famous and quite ancient tea of Húběi, this one goes all the way back to the Tang, is Ēn'shī Yù Lù. This comes from south of Yíchāng at the bottom of Hubei, on the Húnán border. Ēn'shī Yù Lù is special because not only is it incredibly old but they use a steaming method to process the tea that stopped being used after the Tang dynasty. Don't let Laszlo Montgomery fool you. I've never tried either of them, but you can buy them on the internet at some of the web stores that sell tea.

23:10 Hunan is the home of the very special Jūnshān Yínzhēn Tea. Chairman Mao also liked this one. It's another yellow tea. And as yellow's go, this one is considered the top one. It's quite similar to Báiháo Yínzhēn tea, one of the best-known white teas from the province that brought us white tea, namely Fujian. Yínzhēn again means silver needle. That means it's an all-bud tea. Jūnshān Yínzhēn

	is one of the top ten famous teas of China. Actually, I think there may be more than ten teas are claiming to be in the top ten. It's grown on Jūnshān Island, located in beautiful and historic Dòngtíng Lake, Dòngtíng Hú.
23:57	The annual production of Jūnshān Yīnzhēn is only about 500 kilos a year. As far as this Tribute Tea's history, it goes back to the Song. I've seen it for $25 for 100 grams. Rare as it may be, it's still affordable.
24:13	I think I've covered most of the marquee teas of China so far. I skipped over a thousand or so and I hope you won't hold that against me.
24:21	If you didn't know anything about the history of tea before you started streaming episode 1, then for sure you have tons of material for that next cocktail party or mixer. I myself went more than half a century before I was seriously turned on to tea. And after more than a decade of testing the waters, I'm all settled in.
24:42	Honestly, I'm not much of a wine drinker. In fact, even to say not much of a wine drinker is an overstatement. All these years I saw with how much passion so many people spoke of wine and of their wine experiences. I never could be a part of that. But now with tea, I've found it's exactly the same.
25:03	And as far as the history of tea goes, I hope you're leaving the table fully satisfied. It really is a great story, especially in the context of that most famous statement about tea, that after water and air, it's the most consumed

THE TEA HISTORY PODCAST BOOK 2
PART 20

substance on the planet. In that context, the story is particularly poignant.

25:21 If it were so easy to figure out the process, then there wouldn't be anything special about tea. It would be like orange juice. Pick the orange, squeeze it in a glass. With *Camellia sinensis* it wasn't so evident. It took a few thousand years to figure out most of the secrets locked inside. But you have to hand it to human beings in general and the Chinese in particular, they sure are good at figuring things out.

25:48 Yeah, the first Neolithic or Bronze Age people who lived where tea trees grew wild all knew these leaves were special. Thankfully China had a nice long history and amidst all the wars, disunity, famines, plagues, rebellions, changes in the dynasties, despite all that, basically the culture always kept chugging along, always moving forward and tea was part of that historical process.

26:17 We saw in these episodes how it really took a while before tea or tú evolved from this bitter brew into the cha beloved of poets. From the time of the mythical Shen Nong to the Tang Taizong emperor was 3,360 years. That means it went from some legend of raw tea leaves purging poisons from Shen Nong's body into a beverage that was so good emperors demanded that the best of every kind there was be sent to him first. It took 33.6 centuries to go from Shen Nong to Lu Yu and another seven hundred years to get from Lu Yu to the Rock Teas of Wǔyí shān. It wasn't easy and all the secrets took their time before they were discovered.

THE TEA HISTORY PODCAST BOOK 2
PART 20

27:06 I can't recommend enough the six-part CCTV documentary series called Yīpiàn shùyè de gùshì. I don't know if it has an English title, but it translates to The Story of a Leaf. This documentary did a great job visually of presenting tea and showing how special it is. I'll have links to that and a whole other bunch of resources for you to explore in the show notes at teacup.media.

27:33 My hope these past twenty episodes was that I could offer you, my good looking and brilliant listeners, a chance to get an appreciation for tea's history. All throughout, I have encouraged all of you who maybe aren't into tea yet, if your interest has been piqued from the episodes presented in this podcast program, the resources out there to guide you and accompany you on your own little tea journey are plentiful and authoritative.

28:00 That is all I have for you for this episode and about the history of tea in China. Let me close in saying that if this podcast inspired you to go learn more about tea, the internet abounds with experts, blogs, videos and resources that can teach you everything there is to know about everything there is to know about tea. And if you want to sample all the teas I mentioned, you're in luck because as long as it's in stock you can get it online delivered fresh to your door.

28:31 Let me close with a tea poem that sort of says it all for me.

 THE TEA HISTORY PODCAST BOOK 2
PART 20

28:36   *Now stir the fire, and close the shutters fast,*
Let fall the curtains, wheel the sofa round,
And while the bubbling and loud hissing urn
Throws up a steamy column, and the cups
That cheer but not inebriate, wait on each,
So let us welcome a peaceful evening in.

28:56   And I wish all of you, my longtime China History Podcast listeners and those of you who were attracted to this Tea History Podcast because of the attractiveness of the topic, I hope you all get to enjoy that peace and serenity from a quiet evening in, enjoying a nice cup of jiǎ, tú, chuǎn, shè, míng, chá, chai, tea or whatever you call it in your language. Enjoy!

29:23   Take care everyone. And I'm hoping you'll maybe consider joining me next time for another exciting episode of the Tea History Podcast.

The Tea History Podcast
Book 2 Part 21

SUMMARY

As Porky Pig used to say, "That's all folks". But only for this Chinese tea history series. I hope you enjoyed this telling of the history of tea.

TRANSCRIPT

00:00 | Hey everyone, welcome back for the twenty-first time. well, twenty-two is you count the trailer. Laszlo Montgomery here once again with another THP episode.

00:10 | This time around, I wanted to sort of recap some of the things mentioned over the past twenty episodes. This is as far as I planned to take this Tea History Podcast.

00:21 | The history of tea certainly is a long one that is intricately meshed with the history and culture of China. Whether this bond actually began in 2737 BCE with Shén Nóng, who is to say for sure? All we can be assured of is that the original tea garden that grew as nature planned it began long before the development of Neolithic civilizations and was located in southwest China and around the Golden Triangle and stretched westward all the way to the Brahmaputra Valley of Eastern India. We know for certain that's where it all began, and always thrived, as it still does today.

THE TEA HISTORY PODCAST BOOK 2
PART 21

01:05 Tea history is longer and older than many of the oldest tea trees that still stand today. Tea trees that are a thousand, two thousand and maybe even three thousand years old are still growing wild, offering silent testament to their long existence.

01:23 Who knows how many thousands of years passed before humankind discovered the merits of this leaf. We can marvel at how the Chinese were the first to discover tea and how to heat it, pound it, bake it, roll it, smoke it, dry it and do whatever it was to create a beverage that would, in time, meet with almost universal acceptance in every civilization who came in contact with it.

01:53 Tea culture didn't just happen in China. Wherever tea went, the people of those lands would enjoy this beverage. After familiarizing themselves with tea, people would swaddle this drink with their own culture and add their unique touch and make it special just for them. This happened wherever tea went.

02:17 Even though I've been rambling on for all these episodes about tea, the truth is I have barely scratched the surface of this subject. What tea means in China isn't necessarily what tea means in Turkey. Every place has their own preferred tastes and unique ways to prepare it and enjoy it.

02:38 If you're interested at all, there's really a whole world to enjoy. For all of you who perhaps haven't sampled tea beyond a Lipton or Tetley tea bag, I hope this series has so far inspired you to maybe go beyond this tried-and-

THE TEA HISTORY PODCAST BOOK 2
PART 21

true brew and sample some of the delights of artisanal loose leaf tea. Yeah, it takes a little more time to prepare, but anyone will tell you, there's a world of difference.

03:06 In the previous episodes, I introduced many of the key people remembered in the History of Tea for various reasons. We went as far back as 59 BCE with Wáng Bāo and that ancient contract that itemized tea as well as other info that revealed an existing tea market in the time of Emperor Xuān of the Western Han.

03:29 The story of Wáng Bāo for centuries was as far back as the tea story went. Then in 2016 tea buds were discovered in the tomb of Han Emperor Jǐng. This isn't necessarily proof of a culture of tea drinking, but it does show they knew about *Camellia sinensis* that far back when this emperor reigned, 157 to 141 BCE.

03:56 During the Western Han, the Chá Zǔ or Tea Ancestor, Wú Lǐzhēn brought those seven tea bushes to Méngdǐngshān in Sichuan around 53 BCE and began the organized cultivation of tea in China for the first time.

04:14 We saw in Part 1 how, in China's case, evidence of tea's development from bitter vegetable to pleasure drink was found in a number of historical documents that showed how far tea had advanced over the history timeline. Each of these surviving works are like pieces of a jigsaw puzzle that showed the progression of how much closer the Chinese were getting over the centuries to achieving a full understanding of tea's secrets.

THE TEA HISTORY PODCAST BOOK 2
PART 21

04:45   The *Shuōwén Jiězì*, as mentioned in Part 1, showed us the character *míng* for tea and explained in the Han dynasty what tea was. As we got deeper and deeper into the Hàn Dynasty, literature that mentioned tea began to become more plentiful. But like anything from two thousand years ago, unless someone carved it in stone or cast it in bronze or if archaeologists got lucky and stumbled into a tomb that by chance had not been plundered, there's very little survives. All we have really, up until the time of the Tang dynasty, are just bits and pieces of these references made to long lost works.

05:28   We also introduced the people in China, rather unknown, who get credited for being the first to make something of tea. These were the people of Bā and Shǔ. These two kingdoms were located mostly in Sichuan province. Today all over the capital of Sichuan, Chéngdū, you can see references to Shǔ everywhere. We looked at the introduction of *gòngchá* or tribute tea. If the tea was good enough for the emperor, you can rest assured that it had reached a stage of refinement and quality others less exalted than the emperor of China wanted taste as well.

06:08   And then once the Suí and the Táng came and went, tea had its first truly great moment on the national stage. That really was the dividing line as far as Chinese tea history is concerned. There was everything before Lù Yǔ in the Táng and then everything that followed. The Táng dynasty brought tea culture to great heights unseen before in China. Successive dynasties would build on the achievements in the Táng and add their particular

166

THE TEA HISTORY PODCAST BOOK 2
PART 21

touch later on. But it was in the Táng where tea and tea culture truly turned a corner.

06:45 And because of the Silk Road that was already many centuries old, traders and Buddhist pilgrims who came to Cháng'ān, the capital, also had their first close encounters with chá as it began to be called.

06:59 We saw how the first ones outside China to get hooked on tea were those closest in proximity to China. From this period in the Tang biānchá or border tea began to be traded. And for a two-way trade to exist you needed something to barter for and a route to get there. I gave a very brief overview of the chámǎ gǔdào, the ancient Tea-Horse Road that you can still see bits and pieces of today.

07:26 I showed how Buddhism cuddled up nice and close with tea from the earliest times. In the Tang and clear through to the Qīng, it was the Buddhist monasteries who would cultivate some of the most prized teas. And in the case of Chán or Zen Buddhism, tea would actually become part and parcel of the liturgy.

07:48 I mentioned a couple times Japan's contribution to tea was so great and far-reaching that I decided not to wade too deep into those waters yet. We looked at the monks Saicho and Kukai who did so much to bring *Camellia sinensis* to the Land of the Rising Sun.

08:06 What tea inspired in literature, painting, ceramics, calligraphy and social customs is a whole massive topic

THE TEA HISTORY PODCAST BOOK 2
PART 21

in and of itself. Although I didn't delve too deep into this aspect of tea, I hope at least I gave you an appreciation of how tea, like wine, served as a muse to inspire so many creative minds to produce works of art from their paintbrushes and ink brushes.

08:33 I read you Lú Tóng's famous poem Qī Wǎn Shī, Seven Bowls of Tea. That was one of countless tens of thousands of these so-called tea poems produced between the Tang and the Qing. And I suppose even in our modern day, poets can't resist writing about tea.

08:52 In later episodes I traced the history of tea in the post-Tang world. In the Tang era, tea for the first time assumed the role in Chinese society as a link between art and life. We looked at Jiàn ware, Xíng ware, and *qīngbái* as a few of the most famous early examples of *chájù* or *tea ware*.

09:12 Then in the Song, tea was ground down into a powdered form and people would *diǎnchá* or whisk the tea and the low and high-born alike would engage in *dòuchá* contests with each other. And even more so than in the Tang, aesthetics and tea joined up in the Song and gave birth to all kinds of ceramic, artistic and literary treasures.

09:36 We also looked at the main *chárén* of the Northern Sòng, Cài Xiāng, who among a long list of achievements gave us the Chá Lù, the Record of Tea. Cài Xiāng took Lù Yǔ's Classic of Tea up to Song Dynasty standards and left his mark as a great contributor to the many tea treatises of imperial Chinese history.

THE TEA HISTORY PODCAST BOOK 2
PART 21

09:59 | The Song was another great dynasty of poets. One of the most revered men of his age was Sū Shì, Sū Dōngpō. He was, among many other things, a great tea expert of his day. He left a lot of tea inspired poems that were recited throughout the ages. And yes, he gave us the braised pork dish, Dōngpō Ròu for which I am forever thankful, though my coronary system might take issue with that.

10:29 | In the Ming, loose tea as we know it in our day and age, became the standard throughout the land by executive order from no less a man than the founding emperor Zhū Yuánzhāng, the Hóngwǔ Emperor.

10:41 | We looked at the Ming contribution to a long line of tea classics. The Chá Pǔ was written by the Hóngwǔ Emperor's apolitical son Zhū Quán. This was followed by another work written by Gù Yuánqìng, one that shares the same name: the Chá Pǔ or Tea Manual or Tea Guidebook.

11:01 | We saw how the Ming let forth a gusher of new tea culture. Jǐngdézhèn became the most renowned supplier of imperial and mass grade ceramics the world had ever seen up to that time. They were practically an arm of the imperial government in Beijing.

11:21 | Yíxīng ware became all the rage during the Ming. We looked at all those zǐshā purple clay items and I mentioned how, for Pǔ Ěrh and Oolong, all the experts swear by this kind of Yíxīng ware. Next time you're in Hong Kong feel free to check out Vitasoy founder K.S. Lo's Yíxīng ware collection located in Hong Kong Park at the Flagstaff House Museum of Tea ware. K.S. Lo was

THE TEA HISTORY PODCAST BOOK 2
PART 21

one of the greatest collectors of these treasures and did a lot to bring back and popularize Yíxīng tea pots in the 20th century.

11:59 Then we closed off our history of tea with the arrival of the Western traders into China's perfect little world. The Portuguese, the Dutch, the British, the French, and after 1783, the Americans as well. Everyone came to China to buy tea. Maybe the market just got too big for China's restrictive export system. So we saw how trouble began when British traders sought out a way to get around this system.

12:29 In the late 1840s and early 1850s, the whole kit and caboodle of how to plant tea, grow it, pick it, process it and shape it into all kinds of different ways, everything, the hardware and the software, it was surreptitiously secreted out of China, loaded on a ship and off to India everything went. And China's export tea industry took a big hit because of that.

12:55 By the time of the roaring '20's there was almost no Chinese presence in Western international tea markets. By then, over a million Indian workers were mass producing the stuff in the mountains and hills of northeastern India. And no small amount in Sri Lanka as well.

13:13 But tea is roaring back and those who like to buy from small-time operations offering the absolute topmost quality can do this online. This is the way to go. And if you're fortunate enough to have access to a teashop in your neighborhood, you can get all kinds of fresh stuff

THE TEA HISTORY PODCAST BOOK 2
PART 21

and a nice variety of China and India teas, and from other places as well. I used to live near a tea shop in Claremont. But I regret they did not survive COVID. But when they were around and when I lived there, they also had teas from Vietnam, Iran Kenya, and other places.

13:50 I hope I piqued your curiosity a little regarding tea. There are a whole lot of tea aficionados out there who have written books, uploaded videos, given lectures and tea ceremony demonstrations. There is no shortage of resources for you to refer to and learn from.

14:12 If you want to dive headfirst into the world of tea, there are a cavalcade of experts and chá dàshī's out there to show you the ropes. And they do it in many languages. Obviously if you can understand Mandarin, you can watch tea videos on Chinese platforms like Yōukù. And as I said, when you start to test out your first artisan loose leaf teas, there are plenty of online shops carrying everything, and everything you might ever dream of having as part of your own personal supply of leaf as well as the equipage.

14:49 That's all I have for ya'lls this time. Thanks everyone for tuning in. This is Laszlo Montgomery signing off from lovely SoCal. I do hope you'll think it over and consider joining me next time, and it won't be too long for another exciting episode of the Tea History Podcast.

THE HISTORY OF TEA
COMPLETE LIST OF TERMS

Pinyin/Term	Chinese	English/Meaning
Āndì	汉安帝	Emperor An of Han, reigned 106 to 125
Anhui	安徽	Province in Central China west of Zhejiang. Capital is Hefei
Ānkāng	安康	China's Land of Folk Songs in southern Shaanxi Province
Ānxī	安溪	City in Fujian north of Xiamen and west of Quanzhou, famous for Tieguanyin Tea
Ānyáng	安阳	City in Northern Henan where the Shang Dynasty Ruins of Yin were located
Bā	巴国	The ancient state of Ba, located in modern Chongqing and Western Hubei
Bā Shǔ	巴蜀	The two ancient states located down in present-day Sichuan province. Shu was centered around Chengdu. Ba was centered around Chongqing
Bā Xiān	八仙茶	A kind of Wuyishan Rock Tea. The "Ba Xian" were known as The Eight Immortals
Bái Háo	白毫	Literally means, "white hair". Also was called Pekoe by the Dutch
Bái Jī Guān	白鸡冠	A type of Rock Tea from the Wuyi Mountain region
Bái Mǔdān	白牡丹	White Peony Tea
Bái yá	白芽	White bud
Báiháo Yínzhēn	白毫银针	Silver Needle tea, also called White Pekoe Silver Needle Tea from Fujian province

Bàn Yán Tea	斑岩茶	Tea that grows in the foothills of the Wuyi Mountains
Bǎojiànpǐn	保健品	Health Products
Bēi	杯	A cup
Běiyuàn tea	北苑茶	Famous tea from Fujian, in brick form, was one of the earliest Tribute Teas. They were later molded into small tea cakes called Lóngfèng Tuánchá 龙凤团茶: Dragon-Phoenix Tea cakes
Biàn	汴	The name of Kaifeng during the Northern Song
Biānchá	边茶	Border tea. Tea that is sold to the border regions of China, including Tibet
Bìluóchūn	碧螺春	Green Snail Spring tea from Jiangsu province
Bǐngchá	饼茶	Tea that has been compressed into a cake form
Bohea	武夷	The term used for black tea from the Wuyi Mountains region, but later adopted for pretty much all black teas no matter the origin
Bùpíngděng tiáoyuē	不平等条约	Unequal Treaties
Cái Jīng	蔡京	1047-1126, Norhtern Song statesman and politician during the reign of Huizong
Cài Xiāng	蔡襄	1012-1067, Chinese politician, engineer, poet, and arguably the greatest calligrapher during the Song dynasty
Cǎichánü	采茶女	Tea pickers (女 means girl). Not all tea pickers are female however
Chá	茶	The character for tea decided on during the Tang Dynasty

Chá Chán Yīwèi	茶禅一味	Tea and Chan Buddhism one taste
Chá Jīng	茶经	The Classic of Tea, Lu Yu's masterpiece that explained tea to the masses
Chá Lín	茶林	Tea Hill, located in northwest Hunan
Chá Lù	茶录	Name of the Tea Treatises by Song Emperor Huizong and the Treatise written by Cai Xiang. Same Chinese names but different texts
Cha no Yu	茶の湯	Another name for the Japanese Tea Ceremony (also Chado—茶道 see below)
Chá Pǔ	茶谱	Tea treatise written by Gu Yuanqing in 1541
Chá Shèng	茶圣	The Tea Saint, Lu Yu
Chá Wénhuà	茶文化	Tea Culture
Chá Xiān	茶仙	A "Tea Immortal"
Cháchéng	茶城	A tea city. Fairly common all over China. Shopping centers where all the units sell tea, teaware and tea accouterment
Chado	茶道	Also known as the Japanese Tea Ceremony
Cháhé	茶荷	A tea scoop used to retrieve the tea leaves from your jar or container
Chámǎ Gǔdào	茶马古道	The Ancient Tea Horse Road that transported tea to the borders of western China in exchange for horses
Chán Buddhism	禅	Chinese school of Mahāyāna Buddhism. It developed in China from the 6th century CE onwards, at Shaolin Temple, becoming dominant during the Tang and Song dynasties. It is known as Zen Buddhism in Japan
Cháng zuǐ hú	长嘴壶	A long spout tea kettle, usually made from copper

Cháng'ān	长安	Located in present day Xian, Shaanxi Province, capital of the Western Han and Tang Dynasties (among other dynasties)
Chāngnán Zhēn	昌南镇	Another former name of Jingdezhen. Some say the term "China" comes from Changnan
Chángshā	长沙	Capital city of Hunan province
Chángxīng	长兴	a county in Huzhou prefecture on the southwest shore of Lake Tai
Chánóng	茶农	A tea farmer
Chánpǐn	产品	product
Chǎoqīng	炒青	a kind of drying perfected in the Ming that used a pan or wok to fry the withered leaves of the freshly picked tea
Cháozhōu	潮州	City in eastern Guangdong, famous for many many aspects of their culture
Chápán	茶盘	A Tea Tray used to carry out a gongfu tea ceremony
Chárán	茶人	A "tea person," someone knowledgeable and expert about all things tea and whose passion for tea knows no bounds
Chéngdū	成都	Capital of Sichuan province and site of the ancient Shu State
Chénghuà	成化帝	Ming emperor who reigned 1464-1487
Chónghuá Palace	重华宫	Palace built in 1727 by Yongzheng Emperor for his son, the Qianlong Emperor
Chóngqìng	重庆	Formerly part of Sichuan, now an independant municipality
Chuǎn	荈	Another Chinese character for tea

Co Hong	公行	a guild of Chinese merchants or hongs, operated the import-export monopoly in Canton (present-day Guangzhou) during the Qing dynasty. They reported to The Hoppo
Cuī Guófǔ	崔国辅	Along with Cou Fuzi, one of Lu Yu's early teachers
Dà Hóng Páo	大红袍	A kind of Wuyi Mountain Rock Tea with a lot of folk tales associated with it
Dà Míng Yǒnglè Zhì	大明永乐制	Made during the reign of the Ming Yongle Emperor
Dàguān Chálùn	大观茶论	The Treatise on Tea, also called General Remarks on Tea
Dàimào zhǎn	玳瑁盏	Tortoiseshell design
Dāncōng	单枞茶	A type of Ooolong tea from Guangdong province
Dàoguāng	道光帝	Qing Emperor from 1821-1850
Dàyè	大叶	Big Leaf
Déhuá	德华	in central Fujian west of Quánzhōu developed quite a porcelain legacy
Dézōng	唐德宗	Tang Dynasty emperor who reigned 779-805
diǎnchá	点茶	a popular tea drinking method in the Song Dynasty that involved "mocha" and a whisk
Dìjíshì	地级市	A prefecture-level city
Dìngcí	定瓷	Produced at the Ding kilns in Hebei province. Ding ware had a white or greyish body and a nearly transparent white-tinted glaze
Dìngzhōu	定州	City located in Hebei, halfway between Bǎodìng and Shíjiāzhuāng

Dòngdǐng	凍頂	Tea that came from around the mountains of Lùgǔ Township 鹿谷鄉, Nántóu County 南投縣 in Taiwan
Dòngtíng Hú	洞庭湖	Lake in northern Hunan at the border with Hubei
Dòuchá	斗茶	A "tea battle" or "tea contest" in which people face off to make the perfect cuppa. This was one of the defining characteristics of Song Dynasty tea culture
Dòuhuāzhuāng	老四川豆花莊	Not sure if it's still around but Lao Sichuan Douhuazhuang was (is) a famous Beijing restaurant serving Sichuan food
Duī	堆	mounds or piles
Duke Huán of Qí	齐桓公	Ruler of Qi State from 685-643 BC
Duke of Zhōu	周公	Son of King Wen, brother of King Wu, a very revered figure in ancient Chinese history
Dūyún	都匀	City in Guizhou located two hours by car west of the capital Guìyáng
Dūyún Máojiān	都匀毛尖	A "Famous Tea" from Guizhou
É'Méi Shān Bái Yá	峨眉山白芽	Another great tea of Sichuan from the Mount E'Mei area
É'méi Shān Máofēng	峨眉山毛峰茶	Yet another great tea of Sichuan from the Mount E'Mei area
Eastern Zhōu	东周	The Eastern Zhou Dynasty, divided up into The Spring & Autumn anbd Warring States Periods. It lasted from about 771 to 256 BC

Eisai	栄西	Myōen Eisai, 1141-1215, a Japanese Buddhist priest, credited with bringing both the Rinzai school of Zen Buddhism and green tea from China to Japan. He is often known simply as Eisai/Yōsai Zenji (栄西禅師), literally "Zen master Eisai".
Emperor Guāngwǔ of Hàn	汉光武	Eastern Han Emperor who reigned 25-57 CE
Emperor Saga	嵯峨天皇	The 52nd Emperor of Japan who reigned 809 to 823. He's famous, among many other things, for being the first Japanese emperor to drink tea.
Emperor Xuān	汉宣帝	Emperor Xuan of Han, reigned 74 to 48 BCE
Emperor Xuánzōng	唐玄宗	Tang emperor who reigned from 713-756
Ēn'shī Yù Lù	恩施玉露茶	This tea comes from south of Yíchāng at the bottom of Hubei
Enryaku-ji	延暦寺	Established by Saichō himself in 788. It was a Tendai monastery located on Mount Hiei, overlooking Kyoto.
Ěr Yǎ	尔雅	The first surviving Chinese dictionary
Fènghuáng Shān	凤凰山	Phoenix Mountain north of Chaozhou where Dancong tea is grown
Fúdǐng	福鼎市	A county-level city in northeastern Ningde prefecture level city, on Fujian's border with Zhejiang province. Some great teas come from this part of Fujian
Fújiàn	福建	Coastal province in China south of Zhejiang, They grow a lot of tea there. Capital is Fuzhou.

Fuk Lam Mun	福林門	A famous longtime restaurant in Hong Kong with locations in Tsim Sha Tsui and Wan Chai
Fúxī	伏羲	Another legendary figure from early pre-history. The first of the so-called "Three Sovereigns"
Fúzhōu	福州	Capital of Fujian province, located on the northern coast
Gài	盖	A lid or cover
Gàiwǎn	盖碗	A lidded tea bowl used for preparing and drinking tea
Gānlù Tea	甘露茶	Gānlù Tea because it was cultivated during the Gānlù Era, one of the seven eras of the Han Emperor Xuān
Gānsù	甘肃	Province in western China. Capital is Lanzhou
Gāolǐng	高领	kaolinite
Gōng Yù	供御	tribute ware, something presented to the emperor
Gòngchá	贡茶	Tribute Tea
Gōngfu	功夫	Means "effort". Therefore Gongfu Tea would be tea prepared using "extra effort"
Gōngfu chá	功夫茶	Congou Tea as well as the process of making carefully prepared tea for onself or for guests.
Gù Yuánqìng	顾元庆	Great Ming era literatus who compiled the Cha Pu (Classifications of Tea) in 1541
Guǎn Zhòng	管仲	720-645 BC, chancellor to Duke Huan of Qi, revered philosopher and official. Also called Guanzi

Guāngcǎi	光彩	Means lustre, splendour, radiance. A kind of porcelain ware famous in the Guangzhou area for its designs
Guǎngdōng	广东	Coastal province in southern China. Guangzhou (Canton) is the capital
Guǎngxī	广西	Province in China just west of Guangdong
Guāngxù Emperor	光绪帝	Qing emperor who reigned 1875-1908
Guǎngyǎ	广雅	Chinese dictionary written during the 3rd century
Guǎngzhōu	广州	Guangzhou city, capital of Guangdong, Sister City to Los Angeles, also known as Canton
Guānyīn	观音	The Goddess of Mercy
Guìdìng Yúnwù chá		Another famous tea from Guizhou
Guìhuāchá	桂花茶	Osmanthus tea
Guìpíng	桂平	City in Guangxi province
Guìpíng Xīshān	桂平西山茶	A type of tea from Guangxi province
Gǔshù	古树	an ancient tree
Hakka	客家	A Han Chinese sub-group originally from the north of China who migrated to the south and ended up mostly in Guangdong, Fujian, Hunan, Guangxi, Taiwan but found elsewhere in China and throughout the world
Hàn Dynasty	汉朝	Dynasty that ran from 202 BCE to 9 CE and again from 25 to 220 CE
Hán Fēizǐ	韩非子	Name of the Legalist philospher and the book of his writings

Hán Gōu	汗垢	The Han Canal, built during King Fuchai's time in the 5th century BC
Hàn Wǔdì	汉武帝	Western Han emperor who reigned 141-87 BCE
Hángzhōu	杭州	Capital of Zhejiang Province. A city of superlatives.
Hànkǒu	汉口	The "Han" in Wuhan. One of the cities that makes up this megalopolis in Hubei Province
Hē chá	喝茶	to drink tea
Hē xīběifēng	喝西北风	To drink the Northwest Winds...to suffer some calamity
Héběi	河北	Province in northern China. The capital is Shijiazhuang. The municipalities of Beijing and Tianjin are both located within the borders of Hebei.
Hēichá	黑茶	Black tea or dark tea like Pu-erh
Hénán	河南	Province in central China north of Hubei. The capital is Zhengzhou
Hóng chá	红茶	Black tea (even though "hong" means red)
Hóng Xiùquán	洪秀全	1814-1864, the one who's to blame for the Taiping Rebellion
hóngchá	红茶	Red tea. But in the West this category is called "black tea"
Hóngwǔ emperor	洪武帝	Era name for the founding emperor of the Ming Dynasty, Zhu Yuanzhang who reigned 1407-1505
Hoppo	粤海关部	the Qing dynasty official at Canton given responsibility by the emperor for controlling shipping, collecting tariffs, and maintaining order among traders in and around the Pearl River Delta from 1685 to 1904.

Hóukuí	猴魁	The Monkey King, for which Taiping Houkui Tea is named
Huāchá	花茶	Scented tea (Jasmine, Orchid, rose, osmanthus etc...)
Huái River	淮河	One of China's great rivers, located in between the Yellow and Yangzi Rivers
Huālián	花蓮縣	County located on the east coast of Taiwan
Huáng shān	黄山	Sacred mountain located in Anhui
Huáng Tíngjiān	黄庭坚	1045-1105, Song Dynasty calligrapher, painter, and poet
Huángshān	黄山	The Yellow Mountain range, in southern Anhui Province in eastern China
Huángshān Máofēng	黄山毛峰	The most renowned tea of Anhui Province (or so it's said). Yellow Mountain Hair Tip
Huáxià	华夏	A term for the many tribes that clustered around the Yellow River and are considereds the most ancient ancestors of the Han Chinese.
Húběi	湖北	Province in central China north of Hunan
Húběi rén	湖北人	A person from Hubei Province
Húgóng Temple	胡公庙	Temple located on Mt. Shīfēng 狮峰山 where the Qianlong Emperor visited and planted eighteen tea trees that went on to produce Longjing Tea
Huìzōng	元惠宗	Yuan Dynasty emperor, the final one, who reigned 1333-1368
Huīzōng	宋徽宗	Second to the last emperor of the Northern Song whose poor leadership led to the fall of the dynasty in 1127. It was reconstituted down in Hangzhou later and lived on as the Southern Song.
Húnán	湖南	Province in central China south of Hubei

Húzhōu	湖州	Located in Zhejiang province on the south side of Lake Tai
Jiǎ	檟	Another ancient name for tea
Jiājìng	嘉靖帝	Ming emperor who reigned 1522-1566
Jiàn ware	建窯	A type of tea ware produced in Jiànyáng 建阳 in Fujian province
Jiāngsū	江苏	Coastal Province north of Zhejiang. Capital of Jiangsu is Nanjing.
Jiāngxī	江西	Province just west of Fujian and Zhejiang. Capital is Nanchang.
Jiǎo Rán	皎然	730-799, Tang dynasty poet and noted Buddhist Monk
Jiāqìng Emperor	嘉庆帝	Qing emperor who reigned 1796-1820
Jiāyì	嘉義縣	County located in southwest Taiwan
Jìn	晋朝	Chinese dynasty that lasted from 266 to 420 CE
Jīn	金朝	The Jürchen Jin Dynasty that lasted 1115-1234
Jīn	斤	a "Chinese Pound", also called a "catty", 1.1 pounds
Jǐnán	济南	Capital of Shandong Province
Jǐngdé	景德	Era name during Zhenzong's reign that gave us the name of Jingdezhen. It lasted from 1004-1007
Jǐngdézhèn	景德镇	City in Jiangxi renowned for their historic kilns and ceramics history
Jīngmén	荆门	City in Hubei
Jīnjùnméi	金骏眉	Golden Beautiful Eyebrow Tea

Jīnshā Spring	金沙泉	A fresh water spring located at Mount Guzhu, where Purple Bamboo tea was grown
Jiǔjiāng	九江	City in Jiangxi province
Jūnshān Yīnzhēn Tea	君山银针茶	A famous tea from Hunan
Jürchen	女真	A Tungus ethnic group, predecessor of the Manchu ethnic group who founed the Later Jin Dynasty (后金) and Qing Dynasty
Kāifēng	开封	Another ancient capital of China, located in Henan province east of Luoyang. Most famously it was the capital of the Northern Song Dynasty from 960-1127
Kāimén qījiàn shì	开门七件事	The Seven Necessities of Daily Living in China. The original six were firewood, rice, oil, salt, soy sauce and vinegar
Kāiyuán Era	开元	Period during Tang Emperor Xuanzong's reign from 713-741
Kāngxī Emperor	康熙帝	Qing emperor who reigned 1662-1722
Keemun Congou	祁门工夫	Keemun tea produced from one leaf and the tea bud
Keemun Háo Yá	祁門豪芽	A type of Keemun tea that is made from a 'fine pluck' which means that the pluck is done early in the season from just-emerging buds.
Keemun Máoféng	祁门毛峰	Keemun tea produced from the two top leaves and the tea bud
Khitan	契丹	Qìdān, Mongol people who ruled Manchuria and poart of north China from the 10th to early 12th century under the Liao Dynasty

King Fūchāi	夫差	King Fuchai of Wu who reigned 495-473 BCE, last king of the Wu State
Kings Wén and Wǔ	周文王/周武王	Kings Wen and his son King Wu, the first two Zhou Dynasty kings
kǔ tú	苦荼	Bitter Tu, or bitter tea
kǔcài	苦菜	a bitter vegetable
Kukai	空海	774-835, inventor of Japanese katakana writing. Buddhist monk, calligrapher, and poet who founded the esoteric Shingon school of Buddhism, the Japanese branch of Vajrayana Buddhism.
Kūnmíng	昆明	Capital of Yunnan Province
Kūnmíng Chá Chǎng	昆明茶厂	The Kunming Tea Factory, where the wodui process was invented
Lake Póyáng	鄱陽湖	Largest feshwater lake in China located in northern Jiangxi
Lake Tài	太湖	Famous lake in China, located in Jiangsu. Many famous cities are located along its shores: Wuxi, Huzhou and Suzhou to name a few
Lántíngjí Xù	兰亭序	The Preface to the Orchid Pavilion, Wang Xizhi's great calligraphic masterpiece
Láo Shān	崂山	Mountain located near Qingdao, Shandong Province
Lǎozǐ	老子	Also known as Lao Tzu, founder of Daoism
Lāsà	拉萨	Lhasa, capital of Tibet
Later Hàn	后汉	Also called The Eastern Han. Ran from 25-220 CE
Lǐ Chūnshēng	李春生	1838-1924, Xiamen-born Father of Taiwan's Tea Industry
Lǐ Jì	礼记	The ancient Book of Rites

Lǐ Qíwù	李齐物	Tang royal family member banished to Tianmen to serve as the new governor
Lǐ Shìmín	李世民	The personal name of the Táng Tàizōng 唐太宗 emperor
Liáng Shíqiū	梁实秋	Also known as Liang Shih-chiu, renowned educator, writer, translator, literary theorist and lexicographer.
Liáo	辽朝	The Liao or Khitan Dynasty 907-1125
Lín Zéxú	林则徐	Qing era official and Viceroy who lived 1785-1850. Considered a national hero for standing up to the Western powers in the 1830's
Língyán Monastery	灵岩寺	Monastery at Tàishān where Master Xiangmo lived and taught
Lìshān Xiǎozhǒng	立山小种	Lapsang souchong tea
Liú Bāng	刘邦	Founder of the Han Dynast, reigned as Han Gaozu
Liú Sòng	刘宋	Liu Song Dynasty 420-479 the first of the southern dynasties during the Southern and Northern Dynasties Period, 420-589 that preceded the Suí
Liú Yìqiān	刘益谦	Shanghai real estate tycoon who shelled out $36 million US to purchase a tiny porcelain cup, 3.1 inches in diameter.
Liùbǎo chá	六堡茶	One of the famous teas of Guangxi that was made famous in Malaysia as a tea for the workers.
Lóngjǐng Chá	龙井茶	Dragon Well Tea, a famous tea grown and produced in Longjing village outside of Hangzhou

Lónggài Temple	龙盖寺	Dragon Cloud Monastery
Lóngjǐng	龙井	Longjing, both a village near Hangzhou and the name of the tea grown there. Called Dragon Well tea
Lù Tíngcàn	陆廷燦	Writer of the Xù Chá Jīng 续茶经, The Sequel to the Cha Jing.
Lú Tóng	卢仝	790-835, Tang literatus and renowned poet, as well as a great lover of tea
Lù Yǔ	陆羽	Chinese tea master and literary figure during the Tang Dynasty. Lived 733-804
Lù'ān	六安	City in Anhui Province that has an exception to the rule for the Pinyin spelling of 六. Famous for, among other things, I'm sure, their Lu'an Melon Seed Tea.
Lù'ān Guāpiàn	卢安瓜片	Melon Seed tea from Anhui province
Luk Yu Tea House	陆羽茶室	Famous tea house and dim sum restaurant located on Stanley Street, in the Central area of Hong Kong, established in 1933.
Luòyáng	洛阳	One of the ancient capitals of China, located in Henan province
Lúshān	庐山	County in Sichuan not far from Chengdu
Lúshān Yúnwù	庐山云雾茶	Lúshān Cloud and Mist
Lúshān yúnwù chá, wèi nóng xìng pōlà, ruò dé chángshí yǐn, yánnián yìshòu fǎ	庐山云雾茶，味浓性泼辣，若得长时饮，延年益寿法	The flavor of Lúshān yúnwù tea is strong and intense. If you drink it for long it is a way to attain longevity. Or so says People's Liberation Army founder Zhu De.
Máochá	毛茶	Raw pu-erh tea that can be turned into "sheng" or "Shu/Shou" Pu-Er tea

Máofēng	毛峰	the bud plus the top two leaves
Máojiān	毛尖	any tea that consists of a bud and a single leaf only, also called "fur tip"
Méitán Cuìyá	湄潭翠芽	Guizhou Emerald Tips, a kind of tea from Guizhou
Méixiàn	梅县	County in eastern Guangdong that is often called "The Homeland of the Hakka people"
Méngdǐng Gān Lù Cha	蒙顶甘露茶	A type of tea that comes from Mount Mengding in Sichuan
Méngdǐng Shān	蒙顶山	Méngdǐng Mountain
Méngdǐng shān Xuěyá	蒙顶山雪芽	Mt. Méngdǐng Snow Buds. Xuěyá means snow bud
Mèngzǐ	孟子	Also known as Mencius, a great philospher from the Ru School
Mǐ Fú	米黻	1051-1107, Northern Song painter, poet, and calligrapher known for his style of painting misty landscapes.
Miàoxǐ Sì	妙喜寺	Miàoxǐ Monastery
Minamoto no Yoritomo	源賴朝	Founder and the first shogun of the Kamakura shogunate of Japan, ruling from 1192 until 1199
Mǐnběi	闽北	Mǐnběi dialect of northern Fujian Province
Míng	茗	Another Chinese character for tea
Míng	明朝	The Ming Dynasty, 1368-1644
míngzhàn	茗战	Another name for a "tea war"
mìsè	蜜色	A "secret color"
Mǒchá	抹茶	Ground powdered tea. called matcha in Japanese

Mount Gùzhǔ	顾渚山	Located near Changxing in Zhejiang Province, it was the site of both Jinsha Spring and the famous tribute tea Purple Bamboo.
Mt. Hiei	比叡山	Mountain in Northeast Kyoto where the Enryakuji is located
Myōan Eisai	明菴栄西	1141-1215, Japanese monk credited with bringing green tea to Japan from China. He also studied the Rinzai school of Chan or Zen Buddhism
Nánběi Cháo	南北朝	The Northern and Southern Dynasties period
Nánlǐng River	南凌河	River in northern Jiangsu, renowned in its day for its high quality water
Nántóu	南投縣	County located in the center of Taiwan
Níngbō	宁波	Major city just south of Shanghai. An economic powerhouse loaded with history
Northern Sòng	北宋	The Northern Song Dynasty 960-1126
Wūlóng / Oolong	乌龙	Wūlóng Tea, a partially oxidized tea that is mighty fine tasting
Ōuyáng Xiū	欧阳修	1007-1072, Song dynasty essayist, historian, poet, calligrapher, politician, and epigrapher, featured in CHP episode 71
Pàochá	泡茶	To steep tea leaves in a teapot
Pǐn	品	To sip (among other definitions)
Pǐn chá	品茶	to sip tea
Píngshuǐ	平水	City in Zhejiang south of South of Shaoxing, where gunpowder tea is said to have originated
Pǐnmíngbēi	品茗杯	A "tea sipping cup" that is part of the gongfu tea preparation
Pǐnzhǒng	品种	kind or type

Princess Wénchéng	文成公主	Princess Wénchéng, niece of Tang Emperor Taizong. Chinese tradition says she brought tea and Buddhism to the Tibetan people following her marriage to their great king Songtsen Gampo
Pu-erh	普洱茶	Pu-erh tea, Fermented tea produced in Yunnan Province, also a category of tea and a taste all its own
Pútián	莆田	City in Fujian located in between Quánzhōu and Fúzhōu
Qī wǎn chá	七碗茶	Seven Bowls of Tea, one of Lu Tong's more famous tea poems
Qī zǐ bǐngchá	七子饼茶	"seven brother tea cakes", a kind of packing method for compressed Pu-er tea cakes
Qiǎn Táng Shǐ	遣唐使	Kentoshi, from the 7th to 9th centuries….607 to 838….Japan sent nineteen embassies to China
Qiāng	羌族	One of the ethnic monority people of China, who live mainly in a mountainous region in the northwestern part of Sichuan on the eastern edge of the Tibetan Plateau.
Qiánlóng	乾隆	Grandson of Kangxi, Qing Dynasty ruler who reigned 1735-1796
Qímén	祁門	County in southeast Anhui Province, famous for their tea and for being the headquarters of Zeng Guofan's Xiang Army
Qín	秦朝	First imperial dynasty of China, founded by Qin Shihuang. Lasted from 221-206 BCE
Qín Shǐhuáng	秦始皇	The first emperor of China and founder of the Qin Dyansty
Qīng	清朝	The Qing Dynasty, China's final imperial dynasty 1644-1911

Qīng Guǎngcǎi	广彩	Also known as "Canton Porcelain" used multiple colors on a white ceramic canvas
Qīngbái	清白	A type of tea ware produced during the Song and Yuan dynasties. Qingbai ware is white with a blue-greenish tint
Qīngchéng Shān Snow Bud	青城雪芽茶	Another great tea of Sichuan
Qīnghǎi	青海	Province in western China
Qīngmíng Festival	清明节	Also known as Tomb Sweeping Day, a traditional Chinese holiday that usually falls in the first week of April. People who observe this holiday show reverence for their ancestors by visiting their graves and "sweeping the tombs"
Qiónglái	邛崃	City in Sichuan southwest of Chengdu
Quánzhōu	泉州	Port city in southern Fujian
Rén	人	A person
Rén duō hǎo bàn shì	人多好办事	A quip by Chairman Mao that means, the more people you have the easier it is to get work done
Rénmín Gongyuan	人民公园	A public park in the city of Chengdu where you can relax and enjoy some decent tea culture
Rénzōng	仁宗	Song emmperor who reigned 1010-1063
Ròuguì	肉桂	A type of Rock Tea from the Wuyi Mountain region
róuniǎn	揉捻	The polling and pounding process of tea-making
Rù and Rén	入 / 人	Two Chinese characters that look very similar. Rù means to enter and Rén means person

Saichō	最澄	Japanese Budhhist Monk who lived 767-822. His visit to China in 804 was instrumental in bringing some aspects of Chiense culture to Japan, including tea and the Tiantai school.
Sānbǎo Shān	三宝山	Mountains which were chock full of feldspar enriched china stone, the other main component in making porcelain.
sānge kǒu	三个口	"three mouths" 口口口 make up the character "pin" 品
Sānguó Zhì	三國志	Records of the Three Kingdoms
Sānmíng	三明	A prefecture-level city in Fujian
shā qīng	杀青	To "kill the green", one of the steps used in tea processing. This one stops the enzymes from turning the tea black
Shāng Dynasty	商朝	Bronze Age dynasty that ran 1600-1046 BCE
Shàntóu	汕头	City in eastern Guangdong
Shǎnxī	陕西	Province in northwest China, west of Shanxi. Often spelled as SHAANXI. The capital is Xian.
Shānxi	山西	Northern province east of Shaanxi. Capital is Taiyuan.
Shānzhài	山寨	a Chinese term literally meaning "mountain fortress" or "mountain village" whose contemporary use usually encompasses counterfeit, imitation products and events and the subculture surrounding them
Shàolín Temple	少林寺	Temple at the foot of Mount Song in Henan where Chan Buddhism and Chinese kungfu was born
Shāxiàn	沙县	Sha County, outside the city of Sānmíng in Fujian province
Shè	蔎	Another ancient name for tea

Shén Nóng / Shènnóng	神农	The Divine Farmer, an ancient mythological figure of Chinese pre-history, credited with (among many other things) the discovery of tea. Later became a deity in Chinese and Vietnamese folk religion
Shén Nóng Běncǎo Jīng	神农本草经	The Shen Nong Materia Medica or Shen Nong Herbal
Shēng Pǔ-Ěrh	生普洱	Raw pu-erh tea that has not ripened or undergone the wodui process
Shénnóng Běncǎo Jing	神农本草经	Shen Nong's Herb Root Classic
Shī Jīng	诗经	The Book of Songs, The Book of Odes, one of the Five Classics
Shì, Zhēn, Cūn	市，镇，村	A City, Town, Village
Shóu (Shú) Pǔ-Ěrh	熟普洱	Also called Shú Pǔ-ěr, means Ripe Pu-Erh
Shòu Méi	寿眉茶	Longevity Eyebrow tea
Shǔ Guó	蜀国	The state of Shu, located in modern Sichuan in and around Chengdu
Shǔ yǔ niǎo zhī lù	鼠与鸟之路	The road of mice and birds, a portion of the Ancient Tea Horse Road that was precarious to traverse
Shǔi Jīn Guī	水金龟	A type of Rock Tea from the Wuyi Mountain region
Shǔixiān	水仙	A type of Rock Tea from the Wuyi Mountain region
Shuōwén Jiězì	说文解字	An ancient dictionary compiled during the Han Dynasty
Sìchuān	四川	Province located in southwest China
Sīmǎ Yán	司马炎	Jin Dyansty founder, known as Jin Wu Di 晋武帝

Sīmáo	思茅	The city of Pu-er was renamed Simao after Liberation but now re-named to Pu-er
Sòng	宋朝	The Song Dynasty that ran from 960 to 1279
Sōng Luó	松萝茶	Sung Lo Tea
Sòng Tàizǔ	宋太祖	Temple name of Zhao Kuangyin, founder of the Song Dynasty
Sōngzàn Gānbù	松赞干布	Songtsän Gampo, emperor of Tibet who lived c. 557 to 649
Southern Song	南宋	The Southern Song that survived the Kaifeng-based Northern Song. It lasted from 1127-1279
Sū Shì	苏轼	1037-1101, Also known as Su Dongpo 苏东坡. One of the most beloved characters from Chinese history. He was a poet, writer, politician, calligrapher, painter, pharmacologist, and gastronome
Sū Shùnyuán	苏舜元	1006-1054, a Northern Song literatus and official during the time of Renzong
Sū, Huáng, Mǐ, Cài	苏黄米蔡	The four great Song calligraphers, Su Dongpo, Huang Tingjian, Mi Fu and Cai Xiang
Suí Dynasty	隋朝	Dynasty that preceded the Tang and ran from 581-617
Suí Wéndì	隋文帝	Founder of the Sui Dynasty
Suí Yángdì	隋炀帝	Second Sui Emperor
Sūn Hào	孙皓	grandson of Sūn Quán 孙权, former king of Eastern Wú who loved to drink
Sūyóuchá	酥油茶	Tibetan yak buttered tea
Sūzhōu	苏州	City in Jiangsu province famous for many things

Tài Hú	太湖	Lake Tài, ithe third-largest freshwater lake entirely in China, after Poyang and Dongting.
Tàipíng Hóukuí	太平猴魁	A green tea grown north of Huangshan in Anhui, a favorite of President Putin I read
Táng Dàizōng	唐代宗	Tang emperor who reigned 762-779
Táng Dynasty	唐朝	Dynasty that ran 618-690 and 705-907
Táng Dézōng	唐德宗	Tang emperor who reigned 779-805
Táng Tàizōng	唐太宗	The Taizong Emperor, one of the co-founders of the Tang dynasty, also known as Li Shimin who reigned 626-649
tèdiǎn	特点	characteristic, distinguishing feature, trait
The Yellow Emperor	黄帝	One of the earliest cultural heroes of the Chinese people and a giant in Chinese mythology
Tiānmén	天门	City in Hubei. The hometown of Lu Yu
Tiāntái Zōng	天台宗	Tiāntái sect of Buddhism that developed in sixth century China. The school emphasizes the Lotus Sutra's doctrine of the "One Vehicle"
tiě	铁	iron
Tiěguānyīn	铁观音茶	Iron Buddha or Goddess of Mercy tea, a kind of Oolong tea from Anxi, Fujian
Tǐeluóhàn	铁罗汉	A type of Rock Tea from the Wuyi Mountain region
Tóng Yuē	僮约	A Contract with a Servant
Tóngmù Village	桐木村	Village located in the Wuyi Mountains, where Jinjunmei Tea is grown
Treaty of Nánjīng	南京条约	Treaty signed in August 1842 that ended the First Opium War.

Tsim She Tsui	尖沙咀	District in Kowloon located on the southern tip of the peninsula
Tú	荼	The character for tea before it was called cha 茶
Tùháo zhǎn	兔毫盏	Hare's fur, considered the best was because Emperor Huīzōng, himself said so
Tuìhuò	退货	To return goods (or merchandise....or tea)
tuóchá	沱茶	Tea that has been compressed into a cake form in a particular way described as "birds nest" shaped
Wǎn	碗	A bowl
Wáng Ānshí	王安石	1021-1086. Song Dynasty economist, philosopher, poet, and politician who attempted far-reaching and controversial socioeconomic reforms known as the New Policies.
Wáng Bāo	王褒	The man charged with negotiating a contract for a servant that proved tea was around back in 59 BCE (see Tóng Yuē)
Wáng Xīzhī	王羲之	303-361, Jin Dynasty statesman, politician and perhaps China's most famous calligrapher. Wang Xizhi was featured in CHP episode 96
Wànlì Emperor	万历帝	1573 to 1620
Warring States Period	战国时代	The Warring States Period 476-221 BC
Wéi Yào	韦曜	Eastern Wu official and literary figure who was a teetotaler

Wénchéng Gōngzhǔ	文成公主	Princess Wénchéng, niece of Tang Emperor Taizong. Chinese tradition says she brought tea and Buddhism to the Tibetan people following her marriage to their great king Songtsen Gampo
Wènchuān	汶川	County ih Sichuan not far from Chengdu that was the epicenter of the 2008 Sichuan Earthquake
Wénrén	文人	A literary figure
Wénzōng Emperor	唐文宗	Tang emperor from 827-840
Western Hàn	西汉	The Han Dynasty ran from 202 BCE to 220 CE. The Western Han from 202 BCE to 9 CE. The Eastern Han, from 25 to 220 CE
Western Jìn	西晋	The Western Jin Dynasty 266-311
Western Xià	西夏	Also known as the Tangut Empire. It lasted from 1038-1227 and was located mostly in Ningxia and Gansu
Wò	涡	to moisten
wòduī	涡堆	A kind of process developed to speed up the ripening process of pu-erh tea
Wú Lǐzhēn	吴理真	Buddhist Monk credited with the cultivation of tea on Mengding Shan. He lived during the first century BCE
Wú State	吴国	The Wu State during the Zhou Dynasty that ran from 12th century BCE to 473 BCE
Wùchéng	婺城	A city in Zhejiang "which grows the tea reserved for the emperor as tribute tea."
Wǔgǔ Xiāndì	五穀先帝	The First Deity of the Five Grains. One of Shen Nong's many names
Wǔhàn	武汉	Capital of Hubei Province
Wūlóng	乌龙茶	Oolong Tea

Wúxī	无锡	City in Jiangsi located in between Suzhou and Changzhou
Wǔyáng	武阳乡	Small town not far from Chengdu where an ancient tea marker existed
Wǔyí Mountain (Wǔyí Shān)	武夷山	Picturesque mountains in northern Fujian famous for all their Buddhist temples and teas, especially Oolongs. The term "Bohea" comes from a pronunciation of Wuyi in the local dialect.
Wǔyí Yánchá	武夷岩茶	Wǔyí Rock Tea
Wùyuán County	婺源县	County in Jiangxi province
Wùyuán Míng Méi	婺源茗眉茶	Famous tea from Jiangxi
Xī	硒	Selenium
Xǐ chá	洗茶	To "wash" the tea
Xià Dynasty	夏朝	A mythical dynasty that lasted approximately 2070-1600 BCE
Xiàmén	厦门	Major port city in Fujian. Also known as Amoy
Xiān Cha	仙茶	the tea of the immortals, another name for Ganlu Tea
Xiánfēng	咸丰帝	Qing Emperor from 1851-1861
Xiángmó	降魔藏	Buddhist monk and Chan Master
Xiǎo Cāo	小操	My longtime listener from Lu'an who introduced me to that city and to Lu'an Guapian Tea.

Xíng ware	邢窑	a type of Chinese ceramics produced in Hebei province, during the Tang dynasty. Xing ware typically has a white body covered with a clear glaze. It was named after Xingzhou in southern Hebei where it was made
Xīnjiāng	新疆	China's largest province area-wise, located in the northwest of China
Xīnpíng	新平	Former name of Jingdezhen
Xìnyáng Máojiān	信阳毛尖	Xìnyáng Fur Tip
Xǐshí Ān	洗石庵	Temple in Guìpíng, Guangxi province built during the early Qīng where Guìpíng Xīshān tea is grown
Xīshuāng bǎnnà	西双版纳	Officially called the Xishuangbanna Dai Autonomous Prefecture, in southern Yunnan
Xiūníng County	休宁县	County in Anhui where Song Luo Mountain is located
Xù Chá Jīng	续茶经	The Sequel to the Cha Jing
Xūn	熏	to smoke (in cooking)
Xūnchá	熏茶	Smoked tea (tea with a smokey flavor
Yǎ'ān	雅安	City in Sichuan southwest of Chengdu
Yán Chá	岩茶	Rock tea or Cliff Tea, from the Wuyi Mountains
Yán chá	岩茶	Rock Tea or Cliff Tea, from the upper part of the Wuyi Mountains
Yán Zhēnqīng	颜真卿	Noted Táng official, calligrapher and all around literatus
Yán Zhēnqīng	颜真卿	Chinese calligrapher, military general, and politician. Lived from 709-785. He had a great influence on Lu Yu

Yǎng hú	养壶	to "raise" or season a teapot
Yáng Jiān	杨坚	Second Sui emperor and grandson of founder Wendi
Yángxiàn	阳羡	Former name of the city of Yíxìng, located in Jiangsu Province
Yángxiàn tea	阳羡茶	Yangxian Purple Bamboo Tea, one of the earliest true Tribute Teas of China
Yángxiàn Zǐsǔn cha	阳羡紫笋茶	Yangxian Purple Bamboo Tea, one of the earliest true Tribute Teas of China
Yángzhōu	扬州	City in Jiangsu Province on the north bank f the Yangzi River
Yángzǐ	扬子江	The Yangzi or Yangtze River, China's longest river that runs west to east, located in the geographic center of China. Northern China was north of the Yangzi
Yátóu	芽头	The buds or sprouts
Yǐ chá dài jiǔ	以茶代酒	to substitute drinking tea instead of wine.
Yíchāng	宜昌	City in Hubei
Yīn Xū	殷墟	The Ruins of Yin where the Shang Dynasty had one of its capitals. Ther famous Oracle Bones of China were found here
Yin Zhen Silver Needle	白毫银针茶	A kind of white tea
Yíng Zhèng	嬴政	Personal name of the first Qin Emperor
Yīpiàn shùyè de gùshì	一片树叶的故事	The Story of a Leaf, a very good documentary about tea from the folks at CCTV
Yìwǔ	易武	A town in Mengla County, Xishuangbanna Prefecture
Yìwū	义乌	City in Central Zhejiang famous for it's merchandise market

Yíxīng	宜兴	A county-level city in Jiangsu famous for many things including its famous Yixing tea ware made from the special clay found in that region
Yǒnglè	永乐帝	Ming Emperor who reigned 1403-1424
Yóu dī	油滴	oil droplets design
Yōukù	优酷	The "Youtube of China", a China-based online video platform
Yù Chuānzǐ	玉川子	Lu Tong's pseudonym
Yuán	元朝	The Yuan Dynasty 1279-1368
Yuán'ān County	远安县	County in Hubei province
Yuǎn'ān Lù Yuà	远安鹿苑茶	Yuǎn'ān is the name of the county in Hubei and Lùyuán is the name of a temple there
yuántóu	源头	fountainhead, source, headwater
Yùchá	御茶	Imperial tribute tea
Yuè ware (Yuèqì)	岳器	Yue ware, an early kind of tea ware prized among aficionados and those who could afford it. As the first fine glazed Chinese wares with no toxicity problems from the glazing, Yue ware begins the classic tradition of Chinese ceramics used for serving food and drinking wine or tea.
Yuèzhōu	岳州	City in Zhejiang, near present day Shàoxīng, just a little east of Hángzhōu. famous for Yue ware
Yúgōu Chá	鱼钩茶	Former name of Duyun Maojian tea. Translates to "Fish Hook Tea)
Yúnnán	云南	Province in Southwest China. Pu-Erh Tea comes from this province
Yúnwù	云雾	clouds and fog or clouds and mist

Zàng	藏族	The Zang ethnic minority, better known as the Tibetans
Zhāng Qiān	张骞	Chinese official and diplomat who made a famous adventure to the west and inadvertently kickstarted the Silk Road. he lived during the Han Dynasty and died in 114 BCE
Zhāngjiājiè	张家界	City in Northwest Hunan where Zhangjiajie National Forest Park is located
Zhāngjiākǒu	张家口	Formerly known as Kalgan, a city on the outskirts of Beijing
Zhào Kuāngyìn	赵匡胤	Founder of the Song Dynasty, also known as emperor Taizu. He reigned 960-976
Zhègū bān	鹧鸪斑	partridge feathers design
Zhejiang	浙江	Coastal province in China, and a rich one at that
Zhēn	镇	A town (as opposed to a village or city)
Zhèng Hé	郑和	1371-1433, Ming dynasty admiral, diplomat and explorer, famous for his Seven Voyages to the West
Zhèng Yán Tea	正岩茶	Tea that grows in the rocks in the highest peaks of the Wuyi Mountains
Zhèngdé	正德帝	Ming emperor who reigned 1506-1521
Zhenghe County	政和县	A county in northern Fujian, bordering Zhejiang
Zhèngshān Xiǎozhǒng	正山小种	Another name for Lapsang Souchong Tea
Zhēnzōng	真宗	Northern Song Emperor from 997-1022
Zhìjī Chánshī	智积禅师	Abbot Zhìjī of Lónggài Monastery, Lu Yu's adoptive father
Zhōngguó chá wénhuà	中国茶文化	Chinese Tea Culture

Zhōngguó Zhìzào	中国制造	Made in China
Zhōu	周朝	Dynasty in China that lasted from about 1046 to 256 BCE. In 771 BCE the dyansty entered a new phase called The Spring & Autumn Period and Warring States Period.
Zhōu Gōng	周公	Duke of Zhōu, son of King Wen and brother to King Wu of Zhou. A revered figure in Chinese culture
Zhōu Tea	洲茶	Tea that grows near the banks of the two main rovers of the Wuyi Mountain area, the Zhoiu and Ba Xian Rivers
Zhòu Xīn	纣辛	The wicked last Shang king, known also as King Di Xin
Zhū Dé	朱德	1886-1976, great Chinese revolutionary and founder of the PLA
Zhū Dì	朱棣	Personal name of the Yong Le Emperor
Zhū Quán	朱权	Brother of Zhu Di, the future Yongle Emperor. Zhu Quan write the Cha Pu
Zhū Yuánzhāng	朱元璋	Founder of the Ming Dynasty. He lived from 1328-1398
Zhǔchá	煮茶	To boil tea leaves to prepare tea
Zhūchá	朱茶	"Pearl" tea. Tea pellets
Zhūgě Liàng	诸葛亮	181-234 AD, Great strategist and statesman of the Three Kingdoms period
Zhūshān	珠山	Pearl Hill, today a district of Jǐngdézhēn, a special ceramics operation was set up there to produce porcelain-ware exclusively for the capital
Zhúyèqīng	竹叶青茶	Bamboo Green tea from Sichuan
Zǐshā	紫砂	Purple clay used in the manufacture of clay teapots

Zǐsǔn	紫笋	Purple Bamboo
Zǐsǔn Chá	紫笋茶	Purple Bamboo Tea
Zǐyáng Máojiān	紫阳毛尖	The most renowned tea in Ankang, Shaanxi Province. Ziyang is a county near Ankang
Zōu Fūzǐ	邹老夫子	Along with Cui Guofu, one of Lu Yu's early teachers

www.ingramcontent.com/pod-product-compliance
Lightning Source LLC
LaVergne TN
LVHW061611070526
838199LV00078B/7237